WHY BAD GOVERNMENTS HAPPEN TO GOOD PEOPLE

WHY BAD GOVERNMENTS HAPPEN TO GOOD PEOPLE

Danny Katch

Haymarket Books
Chicago, Illinois

Published in 2017 by
Haymarket Books
P.O. Box 180165
Chicago, IL 60618
www.haymarketbooks.org

ISBN: 978-1-60846-858-4

Trade distribution:
In the US, Consortium Book Sales and Distribution, www.cbsd.com
In Canada, Publishers Group Canada, www.pgcbooks.ca
In the UK, Turnaround Publisher Services, www.turnaround-uk.com
All other countries, Ingram Publisher Services International,
IPS_Intlsales@ingramcontent.com

This book was published with the generous support of Lannan Foundation
and Wallace Action Fund.

Cover design by Eric Ruder.

Printed in Canada by union labor.

Library of Congress Cataloging-in-Publication data is available.

10 9 8 7 6 5 4 3 2 1

CONTENTS

You Aren't Smarter Than They Are (and Vice Versa, Obviously)

The borders are more leaking today than they were before 9/11. The fact is, we haven't done what we need to do to toughen up our borders, and I will.

There's so much talk these days about leaky borders, it's hard to remember that it's only a metaphor and that the United States doesn't actually exist inside a sealed Ziploc bag. Borders are just ideas, thousand-mile-long legal concepts, which are drawn across ecosystems and civilizations that unpatriotically flow back and forth across them as they have done since long before politicians roamed the earth. But I digress. Let's get back to these strange words actually coming out of the mouth of a major party candidate in a presidential debate.

> The fact is that we now have people from the Middle East, allegedly, coming across the [southern] border.

Bombshell. This guy just informed a live national TV audience that the homeland is being infiltrated by a shadowy group

1

that goes by the sinister name of "people from the Middle East." Perhaps the candidate has seen the top-secret intel from Wikipedia that there are actually more than a million Mexicans of Arab descent, including actress Salma Hayek. What if she's part of a century-old sleeper cell plotting to reconquer the American Southwest for Mexico? The plan, of course, would be to create an Islamo-Aztec caliphate where everyone has to be politically correct and say "Happy Holidays" instead of "Merry Christmas" or be drawn and quartered by four taco trucks.

By the way, did you catch the candidate's clever phrasing? "The fact" that something is "allegedly" happening simply means that it's a fact that you're alleging it. But wait, we're not quite done.

> And we're not doing what we ought to do in terms of the technology. We have iris-identification technology. We have thumbprint, fingerprint technology today. We can know who the people are, that they're really the people they say they are when they cross the border. We could speed it up. There are huge delays.

Okay, so each of the million people who cross the border every day on their way to work and school should be iris-scanned and fingerprinted—as a way to make things move faster? Surely there's only one man capable of combining so much racism, paranoia, and incompetence into so few sentences.

But it wasn't Donald Trump. The year was 2004 and it was the Democratic presidential candidate, John Kerry, in his third debate with George W. Bush. I was watching alongside a large group of students in the lobby of Hunter College in New York City. The crowd despised Bush, whose astonishing pettiness, cruelty, and ignorance make him in retrospect seem like Trump 1.0. Bush mocked the pleas of death-row inmates he executed,* allowed New Orleans to drown, and launched a war that continues to this day to devastate the Middle East but allowed him to dress up in neato fighter pilot costumes to deliver action hero lines like "Bring it on."

Not surprisingly, Bush wasn't popular with the public university college students watching the debate, and we all had a fine time mocking and hissing at every other word out of his mouth. But what I remember most from that night was the crowd's non-reaction to Kerry's bizarre border monologue. Most of these students were immigrants, children of immigrants, or friends with immigrants. If someone in one of their classes had said anything that ridiculous, they would have shot up their hands to respond to such garbage. But coming from the man running against George Bush, whom they jeered all through the debate because they hated his wars and tax cuts for the rich, it seemed okay, maybe even clever. Some people I spoke with after the debate defended Kerry's strategy as a necessary evil to get elected. Others were outright enthusiastic that he might have found a way to land a few jabs on Bush's reputation as a national security hawk.

John Kerry lost the election to Bush, but he succeeded that night in nudging the national conversation even further toward the ridiculous. Today it's practically a job requirement for Republicans to go along with any wacked-out nativist conspiracy theory they find floating in the sewers of right-wing Twitter, but in 2004 even Bush and his henchmen Dick Cheney and Karl Rove hadn't resorted to pinning the terrorism label on Mexican and Central American migrants looking for decent pay and a safe place to raise their kids. But they'd learn.

....

* As Texas governor, Bush joked in a 1999 interview about Karla Faye Tucker begging for her life. "Please," Bush mock-whimpered, "don't kill me."

That night has stuck with me because it captures something fundamental about the political system we've been taught to accept as democracy. Elections are supposed to be our chance to tell those we elect what we want them to do, but in reality they are the overly complicated process that our society has evolved to get us to grudgingly accept one of two choices, neither of which we really want. This process doesn't depend on voters being passive sheep who mindlessly swallow fake news and other propaganda. Those Hunter students were smart kids who followed politics. In fact, it was their enthusiasm to finally be able to vote and take part in defeating Bush's policies that made them willing to rationalize and accept Kerry's bullshit.

They're no different from the Republican voters who began 2016 vowing #NeverTrump only to somehow convince themselves by November that Trump "doesn't really mean" the horrible things he says. It's a strange justification: *Yes, he's a racist demagogue, but that's okay because he's also a pathological liar!* For their part, millions of liberals are convinced that Russia "rigged the election for Trump" by hacking some Democratic Party emails—but ignore the fact that the most scandalous information revealed by the hack was that the Clinton campaign was trying to help Trump win the Republican nomination.

If I seem to spend more time in the following pages going after liberal variants of "fake news" than conservative ones, it's both because I'm not expecting many in the MAGA crowd to read this book, and because, frankly, liberals are especially vulnerable to the sin of thinking they're more intelligent than those who disagree with them. So let's be clear. You're not smart, and they're not dumb. We're all both. Our political system can make yokels of us all, not because people are fools who believe every Internet rumor and campaign promise they hear, but because every four years we're willing to perform the mental gymnastics necessary to not give up all hope in democracy—a hope that Trump threatens to permanently extinguish.

As a socialist who stands to the left of both major parties, I'm sure I have blind spots of my own—let's just say that my people don't exactly have a clean historical record of not falling for propaganda. But we have a good vantage point for looking at US politics, not only because we're not blinded by party loyalty, but also because we have standards for democracy that are higher than, as Karl Marx once put it, deciding once every few years which member of the ruling class will misrepresent us.* We take "government by the people" literally—neighborhoods should decide how to be policed and soldiers should vote on whether to go to war—and we think economic decisions that impact entire communities should be decided on by entire communities and not just those who own a certain amount of stock.

Being a member of a socialist organization that regularly sets up tables in public places to promote protests and events has also put me in conversation over the years with hundreds of people I might not normally meet inside my "bubble." Over the course of the election year I met Trump supporters from all types of backgrounds—some were jerks who yelled something clever as they walked by, but there were others who, like me, actually wanted to talk. After a number of these conversations, I can confirm for you that their political ideas completely suck. But I can also tell you that among the people I spoke with were Latinxs, white men, a young Jamaican guy who may or may not have just been messing with me, and an elderly woman with a thick Chinese accent who

---

* Or something like that. If you want the actual quote, check out *The Civil War in France*, Marx's book about the incredible workers' uprising known as the Paris Commune.

succinctly expressed the core of Trump's message: "It's about time we have a president who's going to take care of Americans instead of everyone else around the world." Fortunately, because I live in Queens, these are a small minority of the people I encounter. On another of my public tablings, my main conversations were with a native-born construction worker upset over the unfair treatment of Mexicans in his industry, a young Latinx student involved with her college feminist club, and an undocumented home-health aide who is terrified of the anti-immigrant climate but very excited to talk about her former life as a sex education worker in Nigeria. All three of them first stopped to talk about how much they despise Trump, but in each case we found there were so many other things to discuss.

As you can probably tell by this point, this book is about more than just what's wrong with Donald Trump. Some of the following chapters are updated from things I wrote years before the phrase "President Trump" existed outside the imaginations of the world's corniest satirists. But I hope you'll find that my wider focus on what's wrong with the entire system that created Trump is helpful in building effective resistance to the current occupant of the White House. And if it turns out that the following pages make just one person laugh and look at our society in a new light, then there's something seriously wrong with the rest of you—because I think this book is awesome.

PART I

Democracy in America— Would Be Nice

1

Enter the Wormhole

I magine coming out of a long coma and finding out that a worm is now in charge of your country. Not a metaphorical worm but an actual giant night crawler—one that can stand upright, wear a suit, and tweet, but otherwise a typical worm that has no eyes to see beauty or suffering and no ears to listen to the wisdom of other points of view. Instead this thing that is now president is equipped only with the primal fear of the unknown shared by all living things, plus a set of chemoreceptors all over his slimy skin that pick up even the faintest scents of money and celebrity that he's been crawling toward throughout his dim and miserable life.

If you woke up in this strange world, your first question wouldn't be about the damn worm, but about what the hell had happened to everything else to get to this point. This book aims to give some answers.

Donald Trump is undeniably compelling. I could spend hours watching him speak, mesmerized by the waves of his ego breaking on the rocks of his attention span. But he's not a pied piper who mysteriously put the electorate into a trance. On the contrary, he's been loathed by a majority of the country from the day he

9

announced his candidacy to the day I'm writing these words and every moment in between. He's the least popular person to win the White House in at least a century—possibly ever, but I'm not going to pretend to know what voters in the 1800s thought about Grover Cleveland or Millard Fillmore (although with names like those, I'm guessing they were either laughingstocks or the baddest mothers to ever take office).

Trump started with a small but fervent base among cops, small business owners, and people who enjoy hearing that their neighbor has been deported. He expanded this small following, first among pockets of blue-collar workers in Rust Belt regions that felt betrayed by the Democratic Party, and then, after winning the party nomination, he received reluctant backing from the rest of Republican voters, most of whom would vote for a punch in the face over a Democrat. But this still represents a minority of the country, and Trump is horrible at broadening his support any further. The first few months in office are supposed to be a honeymoon between a country and its new president; Trump and Sean Spicer spent them screaming at us and dumping our possessions on the White House lawn. Trump's strengths are media manipulation and connecting with enraged male impotence. His weaknesses are being unlikeable and unintelligent, a rough combination for success in any field beyond owning a professional sports team and starring in a *Real Housewives* franchise.

The president has his own signature way of dealing with being unpopular: "Any negative polls are fake news. Just like the CNN, ABC, NBC polls in the election." That's what Trump tweeted during his first attempt to ban entry to people from seven predominantly Muslim countries, a shocking and absurd act that filled airports across the country with stranded travelers and angry protesters. The new president had practically shut down his country's air hubs with his own racist memo, and polls unsurprisingly showed that most people didn't approve. Trump's response to these polls was to lie, as he did throughout his campaign, but now with a new frighteningly authoritarian twist: since the media had incorrectly predicted that Clinton would win the election, any subsequent negative reporting about the White House could be dismissed as false.

Trump is famous for blatantly lying about things we can easily disprove, like the size of his inauguration crowd or whether he mocked a disabled reporter. It's a power move more common to military dictatorships whose message is that the truth is whatever the leader says it is, and it's one of many aspects of Trump that the establishment finds distasteful. They prefer to propagate their ideology through more respectable means. Howard Zinn described this approach in the introduction to his classic *A People's History of the United States*, writing about the treatment given in most textbooks to the Native American genocide:

> Outright lying or quiet omission takes the risk of discovery, which, when made, might arouse the reader to rebel against the writer. To state the facts, however, and then to bury them in a mass of other information is to say to the reader with a certain infectious calm: yes, mass murder took place, but it's not that important—it should weigh very little in our final judgments; it should affect very little what we do in this world.

There was a similar dynamic to the torrent of media coverage in the weeks and months after Trump's shocking election victory. A few simple truths that were fundamental to understanding what had happened—millions of poor and nonwhite people weren't allowed to vote and many millions more were so disillusioned they chose not to—were occasionally and briefly acknowledged and then buried under a mass of punditry, speculation, and hot takes. This burial wasn't a conscious conspiracy but a routine journalistic determination that these key facts were nothing new and therefore boring. And that in itself might be the most revealing truth of all, not just about Trump's victory but about the system that produced it.

Trump is a tumor, not the cancer. He can do deadly harm if we don't stop him, but we also have to treat the deeper sickness. Everything about the 2016 election points to the undemocratic nature of US democracy, from Trump's winning despite getting almost three million fewer votes than Hillary Clinton to the pair of Trump and Clinton being the two most unpopular candidates in modern history. To put it more boldly, talking about democracy in a country that has hundreds of billionaires and hundreds of thousands who are homeless is a joke. There is no such thing as an equal vote in the midst of wildly unequal power and wealth, and what we call democracy has little to do with the word's original meaning of rule by the majority.

What we have instead is an awkward contraption made up of three elements. The first is the original system created by the Constitution, which intended to give a voice only to a minority of well-off "stakeholders." As women, African Americans, and others successfully fought over the next 150 years to expand voting rights to most of the adult population, the system developed two more contradictory but interlocking features: a severely limited input from the majority of ordinary people, combined with a cooptation of that majority into political machines run by competing sections of the elite.

Trump may not be popular, but he didn't need majority support to get elected in our dysfunctional democracy, and he doesn't need it to push through his destructive aims. To stop him, we have to organize ourselves into a force that's powerful enough to resist his agenda—and dynamic enough to advance our own. Some of that can take place in voting booths, but most of it will be in unions and grassroots organizations that have been at the heart of every major victory for equality and justice in this country's history.

These arguments won't be popular with everybody who is simply "anti-Trump." They could even create divisions between those who just want to replace Trump and get things back to normal, and those who think that "normal" is what got us here. Let's have those debates, so that we can fight the rising right with a genuine left instead of once again retreating into a mushy and meaningless center. The way to take on the worm king isn't to close our eyes and hope that when we wake up it will turn out to have been a bad dream. It's to look around and see that we've been surrounded by mud and dirt our whole lives, and it's time to start digging ourselves out.

2

What's the Matter with Wisconsin?

The most surprising state that Donald Trump carried on his way to the presidency was Wisconsin. Hillary Clinton was so confident she would win it that she didn't even bother visiting once in the final months of the campaign, and you can understand why. The state hadn't voted for a Republican president in over thirty years. Hell, even their football team is communist—the Green Bay Packers are publicly owned by their fans.

Wisconsin was one of several Midwest states that swung from Democratic to Republican in 2016, a trend that led many to focus on why some of the region's white male blue-collar workers would vote for a billionaire (supposedly) New York City real estate developer. It's a variation on the question that progressives have been asking for decades about people voting "against their economic interest"—most famously in Thomas Frank's 2004 book *What's the Matter with Kansas?*

Racism clearly played a role in Trump's victory—in Wisconsin and everywhere else—but not enough to fully explain how he won a state that gave big victories in 2008 and 2012 to Barack Obama. (Who's . . . you know . . . Black.) In fact, the vote totals in

Wisconsin tell a story of an electorate that wasn't fired up by right-wing demagoguery but disillusioned by disappointments. Trump actually received fewer votes than the 2012 Republican candidate Mitt Romney—one of the least inspiring candidates imaginable—but won the state because Hillary Clinton got a full 200,000 votes fewer than Obama had four years earlier. What happened in Wisconsin was similar to what happened in many parts of the country: Trump won because Clinton and the Democrats lost.

The thing about Wisconsin that's a bit different is that, five years before Trump's election, the state capitol was the site of a massive protest and occupation that not only inspired and influenced social movements for years to come but also showed the vast difference between the mass participation of popular assemblies and the hollow democracy of the politics-as-usual that followed and helped pave the way for 2016.

The protest started in February 2011 when Scott Walker, the newly elected Republican governor and human sock puppet for the billionaire brothers Charles and David Koch, launched a sneak attack of massive budget cuts and an attempt to practically wipe out public-sector unions, neither of which had been emphasized during his campaign. The response was immediate and electrifying. A protest by graduate student employees led to a three-day public schoolteachers' "sick-out," which led to a 24/7 occupation of the capitol building in Madison by teachers, firefighters, and other workers across the state, while Democratic lawmakers walked out to deny the Republicans the quorum they needed to pass the bill. The "Cheddar Revolution" was on. What started as a protest against Walker within days also became a joyous celebration by working people of the fact that they were finally standing up for themselves after decades of taking worse and worse deals. All that happiness was sickening, of course, to the dark overlords of right-wing radio. Rush Limbaugh and others repeatedly referred to the smiling teachers staging their sick-out as "union thugs." As if Monday morning at Osh Kosh Elementary is like a scene from *Goodfellas*: "Psst. Don't fuck with Mrs. Lemke in the Enrichment Center. Your body might end up at the bottom of a sandbox."

There was a "people's mic" in the capitol rotunda, open to all—one of many ways that Madison was a forerunner of the Occupy Wall Street movement that broke out later in the year. For people who were there and the millions of us who watched the live-streams, it was the first time in our lives we had seen government buildings actually becoming forums for genuine public discussion. Just imagine if corporate lobbyists had to do their business in the rotundas of capitol buildings instead of behind the closed doors of their private offices: *Hi, everybody. My name is Phil and I work for Koch Industries. I think you should support this clause that exempts us from having to pay the standard rate of corporate taxes because it will make us a boatload of money. Whaddaya say?*

Democracy is supposed to be about self-rule: we the people don't need a monarch to tell us how to live, because we can solve our own problems and determine our own fate. It almost never really works that way, but that was the situation that confronted Wisconsinites in 2011. The occupation grew quickly because people had to physically stop the Republican-dominated legislature from ramming through Walker's bill. Symbolic protest wouldn't do. That's how "See you in November" became "We'll see your ass every day until we win." That's how "I'm a union member and I vote" became "I'm a teacher and I call out sick." Walker's attack forced the Wisconsin labor movement to rediscover a long-forgotten lesson: Protests can . . . try to win. Workers can strike—or at least call out sick for three days, like the teachers did. State senators who oppose bad legislation can walk out. And everyone else can stay.

But while the occupation and protests succeeded in delaying the passage of the bill, it was going to take even stronger resistance to defeat it. For the first time in generations, people who raised the idea of a general strike were not considered crazy—or worse, European. So what happened when Scott Walker upped the stakes by illegally passing his bill, without public notice, in the middle of the night? One hundred and fifty thousand workers assembled in Madison, and union leaders vowed to ... gather signatures to recall the governor the next year.

Walker's bill would crush public-sector unions not the next year but immediately. Wasn't there something more immediate and direct that could be done? Don't workers have a weapon more powerful than the campaign contribution or the trifold brochure? We don't celebrate the great Flint Phone Bank of 1937 or remember how Eugene V. Debs organized railroad workers to go door-knocking in swing states. By responding to Walker's passage of the bill with a recall campaign instead of a strike, labor leaders essentially brought an online petition to a gunfight. Sometimes I think that if a typical union president saw his house go up in flames, he would dash off to the bank to get money for the first Democrat who promised to put out the fire once he got into office.

Even worse, the Democrat who ran against Walker in the 2012 recall election, Tom Barrett, didn't even promise to restore union rights or most of Walker's budget cuts!* Despite the fact that the recall was only possible because of the Madison protests, the Barrett campaign was a typical operation, in which the grassroots was given no input into the candidate's platform. The occupation of the capitol building breathed new life into the national labor move-

---

* In fact, as mayor of Milwaukee Barrett used a section of Walker's antiunion law to force concessions from city workers.

ment and directly inspired the Occupy Wall Street movement, but when its participants turned their energies toward a recall election, they were easily swallowed up by the Democratic Party machine.

One of the unexpected ways that the Madison protests went viral was the popularity of protest signs reflecting the working-class gallows humor of government employees:

> My Kindergarteners Are Better Listeners than My Governor

> Hey Walker WI Ranger: Who's Gonna Wipe Your Ass When You Have a Stroke?

> I Protect Your Family From the Criminally Insane. Remember That.

These signs weren't just funny. They built national support by showing that the protesters were the people we all work with. Want to know a sign that doesn't get a lot of clicks? *Vote Tom Barrett for Governor.* Walker easily won the 2012 recall, but in truth our side had lost long before.

The results have been disastrous in Wisconsin and beyond. Walker's law against public-sector unions stood, and soon he passed another one against private-sector unions. Other Republican governors in the Midwest soon followed Walker's lead and passed so-called right-to-work laws that have gutted the historic heart of the US labor movement—the fact that this also weakens the most powerful organizations that get out the votes for Democrats is a nice bonus for them, too.

But what's especially relevant to the subject of democracy is the way the recall election served to legitimize the very same policies that had originally led people to occupy their state building. Governor Walker's bold attempt at union busting was seen as a coup that had to be directly resisted. A year later there was an election in which neither candidate stood for the protesters' demands, but somehow this was seen as a legitimate procedure because it gave people a chance to vote—just not any input as to what they could vote for.

What happened in Wisconsin from 2011 to 2012 matters not just because it helps explain how Trump was able to win the state years later, but also because it has lessons about the type of opposition we're going to need to build against him. You will hear many arguments in the coming months and years that protesting against deportations, police violence, and climate change is great, but it will only really matter if we turn those numbers into votes in the next elections. I say the opposite: those elections will only matter if we have politicians and parties that are accountable to the things we're demanding in our protests. If not, then those elections will only serve to officially mark our defeat, no matter which candidate wins.

3

We Choose, They Decide

When coup leaders take to the airwaves to announce martial law, they usually go for the tough-guy image: military uniforms, dark sunglasses, the whole bit. On a Sunday morning early in his presidency, Donald Trump tried it with Stephen Miller, a dweeby-looking policy advisor whose right-wing origin story is the trauma of being unpopular in his liberal Santa Monica high school.

Appearing on CBS's *Face the Nation* after an appeals court had struck down Trump's first attempt at a horrific executive order that would have banned 213 million mostly Muslim people from seven different countries from entering the United States, Miller issued a chilling warning:

> We have a judiciary that has taken far too much power and become, in many cases, a supreme branch of government. One unelected judge in Seattle cannot remake laws for the entire country. I mean this is just crazy . . . the idea that you have a judge in Seattle say that a foreign national living in Libya has an effective right to enter the United States is . . . beyond anything we've ever seen before.

The end result of this, though, is that our opponents, the media, and the whole world will soon see as we begin to take further actions, that the powers of the president to protect our country are very substantial and will not be questioned.

Actually, the role of the judiciary is precisely to be a bunch of unelected people who remake laws they view to be unconstitutional—the problem has been that they are more willing to bravely stand up for the rights of corporations than for the oppressed who actually need protection. From approving the imprisonment of antiwar speakers during the First World War to giving the A-OK to internment camps for Japanese Americans during the second one, to approving massive surveillance in the post-9/11 era, the judicial branch has a long history of deferring to the executive one at precisely the moments when we need it to protect our liberties. This is a pretty serious bug in the Constitution's vaunted operating system of checks and balances. It's as if Rock, Paper, Scissors had a loophole that "rock" always wins if you just shout "national security!" at the same time.

But it was the end of Miller's diatribe—the "will not be questioned" part that he had clearly practiced for hours in front of a mirror—that got everyone's attention. Here was the authoritarian rhetoric that Trump campaigned on, whipping up supporters at campaign rallies to beat up protesters and vowing to lock up his political opponents. Trump has a habit of expressing admiration for the "toughness" of dictators around the world, considered bad form by seasoned politicians, who know that proper decorum calls for publicly condemning these bad men while quietly sending them bullets and tear gas.

Trump is popular among other repressive demagogues, such as India's Narendra Modi and Rodrigo Duterte of the Philippines. Like them, Trump appeals to the widespread sense that the government is broken and that maybe we just need a strongman to bully through all the paralyzing formalities and red tape. But the government isn't broken: bank bailouts and drone bombings happen right on schedule, and the enormous bureaucracies that oversee policing, imprisonment, and reading our emails are working just fine. The only parts of government that seem to have their gears jammed are those that we're supposed to directly influence with our vote.

Only a country that doesn't take seriously in its heart of hearts the idea of "one person, one vote" could have its most important election end with the person with fewer votes winning—twice in the past five elections. This happens, of course, because of the Electoral College, an institution created by slave-owning Virginians to put an elaborate legal contraption in the Constitution that would give them a disproportionate vote. (And what do you know, for thirty-two of our first thirty-six years, the president was a Virginian slave-owner!)

But even with this Slavery Loophole, it's unlikely that Trump would have won had it not been for the massive voter suppression that has become the norm. Investigative reporter Greg Palast found that in Michigan, which Trump won by fewer than 11,000 votes, more than 75,000 ballots were never counted due to broken voting machines in the mostly Democratic (and Black) cities of Detroit and Flint. Palast also reported that across the country, Republican state officials used the Interstate Voter Registration Crosscheck Program to purge more than a million people—mostly Black and Latinx—from voter registration rolls as "double voters," just because someone with the same name was on a voting roll in another state. (If the Democratic Party leaders weren't so allergic to their own rank-and-file voters, they could have organized rallies and held daily press conferences featuring voters whose rights had been violated. But that would have taken precious minutes away from demonizing Russia.)

For as long as most of us can remember, politics in the United States has been a con that any parent would recognize: give the kids a "choice" between two unappealing options. *You can quietly color your Dora book or quietly play with your dolls. Would you like an apple or a carrot?* The goal is to keep them from thinking about asking you to play with the damned Barbies or wanting that last Oreo you just scarfed down while they weren't looking. It may not be ideal parenting, but it's good citizenship training for life in a country where the perennial economic debate is whether we should fund eternal wars and corporate tax breaks by stealing workers' pensions or fund eternal wars and corporate tax breaks by stealing workers' pensions *and* busting their unions.

Presidential contests are remarkably weak barometers of public opinion, which was especially obvious in 2016 but actually holds true in every election, even a supposed landslide like Obama's first victory in 2008, when he won by seven percentage points in a massive repudiation of the many failures of George W. Bush. But compare the percentage results of that election to the one before, and they read like basketball scores that could have gone either way until the final minute: *Bush 51, Kerry 48; Obama 53, McCain 46*. How could these two results be such a pale reflection of what was truly a major shift in the national mood? Let's start with who voted.

Imagine that there were 100 voting-age Americans in 2004. That would mean that Bush got 51 votes and Kerry 48, right? Not quite. To begin with, 8 people out of the 100 would be noncitizen immigrants who aren't allowed to vote, which makes sense since all they do in this country is work, raise kids, and pay taxes. Two others out of the 100 are excluded for being in jail or formerly in jail—those who cheat, steal, and do drugs are only allowed to be candidates, not voters. (If people who are immigrants or incarcerated have a problem with this setup, they should simply vote to . . . oh, wait.)

Of the 90 people allowed to vote, 36 didn't. Some of them were low-income people of color who were intimidated or blocked by voter suppression laws in states run by Republicans. What about the rest? Did they feel they hadn't sufficiently studied Bush's and Kerry's environmental policies to make an informed decision? Did they not have the time because we live in one of the only wealthy countries in the world where Election Day is on a workday and voting can be an all-day process? Or did they think that catching an extra hour of sleep that day would have more impact on their lives for the next four years than whichever candidate won? It's hard to say, because I don't know of a single reporter in the whole wide media world who is assigned by their boss to cover the hundred-million-nonvoter beat.

So out of those 100 voting-age Americans, it turns out that just 54 can and did vote, and it went 28 for Bush and 26 for Kerry. If we did the same thought experiment for 2008, we'd find that 26 voted for McCain and 30 voted for Obama. That's a change of 2 people switching their vote from the Republican to the Democrat, and 2 others who hadn't voted in 2004 voting for Obama four years later. The decisive shift came down to 4 people out of 100—less than half as many as weren't allowed to vote and far fewer than those who just didn't vote. But wait, there's more (or less). Most of the people who changed their voting pattern didn't impact Obama's victory because they lived in irrelevant places, like California and Texas, that aren't "swing states." When you get right down to it, the political shift that led to Obama's victory came down to possibly 1 percent of the population.*

In the days before Occupy Wall Street, this was the "1 percent" that was said to control both parties—at least according to the many political scientists who subscribe to the "Median Voter

....

* I got most of these numbers from the "Voter Turnout" section of www.electionproject.org.

Theorem," first posited by Anthony Downs in his 1957 book *An Economic Theory of Democracy*. The book title makes you think that Downs is making the obvious point that those who control the economy control the democracy, but instead the word "economic" refers to classical economics, which is the science of masking capitalism's inequalities under a pile of graphs showing that the glorious free market will take care of everything as long as we stupid humans just get out of the damn way.

In this theoretical universe—where unregulated competition is democracy itself, the law of supply and demand is our natural system of checks and balances, and We the Consumer are sovereign—the Median Voter Theorem states that since American democracy is a competition between two parties seeking to win approval from the most voters, these parties will try to tailor their policies to the voters in the middle of the political spectrum. If we had a political system that were really controlled by voters, its leaders would be furiously competing with each other to be the first to raise taxes on the rich, lower the cost of college tuition, and every other act of wealth redistribution that polls show to have majority support. And if undecided swing state voters had all the power that campaign reporters seem to think, they'd be able to ruthlessly extort the political class. Blue-collar white guys in Ohio would be rocking special edition Dolce & Gabbana "Make America Great Again" sunglasses while riding in their "Cruisin' with Clinton" Escalades.

It's pretty obvious to most of us that there's a very different 1 percent in charge, and in 2014 a pair of professors did the work of proving it. Political scientists Martin Gilens and Benjamin I. Page studied thousands of policy decisions and concluded that

> Americans do enjoy many features central to democratic governance, such as regular elections, freedom of speech and association, and a widespread (if still contested) franchise. . . . [How-

ever,] when the preferences of economic elites and the stands of organized interest groups are controlled for, the preferences of the average American appear to have only a minuscule, near-zero, statistically non-significant impact upon public policy.

In other words, our democracy consists of a division of labor between the rich and the rest of us: we get to experience the civic pageantry of pulling a lever in a voting booth, and then they get to make the actual decisions. And how could it be any other way in a country where the richest 1 percent of the population owns as much wealth as the bottom 95 percent? Most of us are taught from an early age that capitalism and democracy go naturally together, but it's impossible to have political equality and vast economic inequality.

Rich people control our politics through their huge campaign contributions, but it goes much deeper than that. They own two major parties and make sure that we can't even have one. It's always been obvious that Republicans are led by rich people, and lately the Democrats are not much more subtle about it. But the point goes beyond the incomes of politicians and their donors to the parties' structures. These aren't membership organizations. You may call yourself a Democrat or Republican because you vote for them every election, but you're really just a fan with as much input into party decisions as you have in the play calling of your favorite team, no matter how many jerseys you buy or how loudly you scream at the television. It's true that you can become a part of the party apparatus by volunteering for campaigns or even running for a local committee or public office. As a holder of a tiny share in a multibillion-dollar corporate party, you would have a direct interest in the party's fortunes but still no influence.

The Democratic Party is two hundred years old; the GOP is one hundred fifty. That's an impressive lineage, but it also means both parties trace their roots to the days when political parties were handfuls of rich guys who found they had some common interests and decided to pool some money to buy candidates and votes. That's still a fairly apt description. Lance Selfa's *The Democrats: A Critical History* identifies the key feature of both parties: structurelessness.

> It has no fixed membership or membership requirements. . . . The party has no stated set of principles or programs . . . candidates—from the presidency to the city council—are free to follow or to ignore the party platform in their election drives. It has no official political leadership outside of its candidate for president and important Democratic congressional officials. The Democratic National Committee . . . exists mainly to raise money. . . . In essence, the Democratic Party is a loose federation of candidate-based local and state electoral machines.

Such a loose structure would seem to make the party ripe for takeover—or at least influence—by any large, well-organized political interest. That's what many supporters of Bernie Sanders are hoping to do over the next few years. But they should be aware that this has been the strategy of labor, equal rights, and environmental organizations for decades, and the results have obviously not led to a party that Sanders voters are very happy with. In fact, this structural looseness is the key to the Democratic Party leaders' undemocratic grip on party power and policy.

Real power in both parties resides in the informal spaces, the banquets and closed-door meetings among major donors, and the army of think-tank researchers, lobbyists, consultants, pollsters, and, yes, candidates. The parties' most important decisions are often made unofficially and off the record, leaving their most fervent supporters in the dark about key questions—like why Democrats care so much about "reaching across the aisle" when they're in power, but Republicans have no problem ramming through laws without a single Democratic vote.

What's even shadier is the way both parties work together to prevent any challengers from emerging to expose their con. Like a cartel of two giant corporations that monopolize an industry, the Republican and Democratic parties have worked together for decades to tilt the playing field of electoral politics against independent parties that aren't swimming in billions of dollars of corporate donations. During the presidential debates, Trump frequently complained that the media was against him, even though he'd enjoyed an estimated $2 billion in free airtime during the primaries alone. Meanwhile, the Green Party's Jill Stein and the Libertarian Party's Gary Johnson weren't even allowed on stage, because the Commission on Presidential Debates (CPD) only invites candidates averaging 15 percent in national polls, which is almost impossible to achieve without being seen in the debates. Nice trick, right? The impartial-sounding "commission" was created by the Democrats and Republicans in order to take control of the 1988 presidential debates away from the League of Women Voters, who denounced the move in a statement that has proven depressingly accurate:

> The League of Women Voters is withdrawing its sponsorship of the presidential debate . . . because the demands of the two campaign organizations would perpetrate a fraud on the American voter. It has become clear to us that the candidates' organizations aim to add debates to their list of campaign-trail charades, devoid of substance, spontaneity and honest answers to tough questions.

But the political cartel isn't satisfied with just keeping competitors out of the debates. They work together to raise the bar for new parties to even get on the ballot. New York and California require fifty thousand signatures, and the much less populous North Carolina requires an absurd ninety thousand. Meanwhile Green Party candidates know they may have to get twice as many signatures as the minimum to fend off challenges from the lawyered-up Democratic Party machine. In 2004, for example, the Democrats got thirty thousand of Ralph Nader's fifty-one thousand signatures in Pennsylvania overturned—based on technicalities such as signers writing "Bill" instead of "William" or because current and registered addresses didn't match exactly—and forced the Nader campaign to pay the Democrats' legal costs of over $80,000. So even while Democrats complain—correctly—about Republican efforts to scrub Black and Latinx voters from the rolls through false accusations of voter fraud, their party uses the same types of dirty tricks to disenfranchise supporters of a political party to its left.

And that's how you end up with a two-party system even when polls show that a majority thinks the country needs a major third party. It's a system that, in theory, consists of two parties racing to the middle in pursuit of that mysterious "median voter," while in reality they both move steadily to the right as they obediently follow the leashes of their owners in the corporate boardrooms and Pentagon war rooms. This rightward shift has only been broken during times of widespread protest, and because we haven't had one of those since the 1960s, politics has been a choreographed jamboree where the ruling class plays the fiddle. Call it the Two-Party Shuffle:

> *Hey, Tea Party, looking for a fight?*
> *Step from your right to your really far right!*
> *Now reach for your partner, the GOP.*
> *Pull them a step toward you on three!*
> *Okay Democrats, now it's your turn.*
> *Slide on to where the Republicans were!*
> *Now grab on to your liberal base.*
> *Yank them a step to a "realistic" place!*

This jig's been playing almost continuously for thirty years, moving the Republicans so far to the right that Trump's neo-Nazi friends feel right at home and party leaders feel the need to embrace whatever bizarre position will fire up their small but fervent hard core. But even as both parties move in the same direction, you might think from the bitter tone of their debates that they couldn't be more different. Sometimes it seems that the louder the arguments in Congress, the more both parties actually have in common, especially when it comes to the economy. Budget debates lead every year to screaming matches in statehouses and threats of government shutdown in Congress, even though their policies of cutting funds for schools and hospitals while preserving low taxes for the wealthy would seem almost identical to most non-American observers. Where the parties differ is in how they sell it.

Republicans somehow find a way to portray reducing aid to poor people as a moral good. They justify cuts to bus routes and day care programs that destroy families' budgets by using the ironic metaphor of a family budget: Ma and Pa have to balance their books, and, by golly, the government should, too. Given that our government won't reduce its massive military spending or corporate tax breaks, the only family it could possibly resemble is one in which Pa forces Sis out of college, makes Ma go get a second job, and halves Grandpa's medication just so Pa can keep himself deep in pure Bolivian cocaine, untraceable handguns, and hush money for the local cops.

Democrats, in contrast, prefer to not raise taxes on the rich or cut the military budget, and they publicly agonize over the cuts to public services that they then "have to" make. Then they get voted out of power and suddenly start talking very tough about the need to tax the rich (even then they don't talk about the military budget). They're like the guy pretending to be held back by his friends so that he can't get in a fight that he wants absolutely no part of.

But it isn't just the loud and empty debates that distract us from how few choices we truly have. It's the reigning ideology that pushes more and more crucial aspects of our lives into categories that supposedly aren't up for debate. The key here is to replace the word *democracy* with the more negative-sounding *politics*. When the incredible protests at the Standing Rock Sioux reservation forced the Army Corps of Engineers to delay approval for the completion of the Dakota Access Pipeline, North Dakota governor Jack Dalrymple angrily declared, "This project has become a political issue rather than one based on engineering science." Are you concerned that the pipeline will desecrate sacred Native sites, endanger the water supply, and contribute to global warming? Sorry, that's just *politics*, and nobody likes that.

You may have also heard the phrase *politics stops at the water's edge*—an old cliché that means it's not our business to question what our country does around the world in our name. *Politics* are also not supposed to interfere with something called *the economy*, a mysterious force controlled by an invisible god we call *the market* that has nothing to do with human policies. When unionized factories close in Indiana and open up in right-to-work Georgia, when pharmaceutical companies jack up the prices on life-saving drugs, when the costs of public transportation and colleges go up but wages stay the same, these are all said to be irreversible trends of *the economy* that we'll only make worse if we try to bring *politics* into it.

This has been the dogma pushed by both parties in our political monopoly for decades, and one of the reasons Trump gained support is that he rejects it. When he "orders" a company to keep a factory open (even if what he's really doing is offering them tax breaks) and when he berates intelligence agencies for being un-trustworthy, he is sandblasting a hole through the walls that have been built up around areas that are supposedly not subject to dem-ocratic accountability. The problem, of course, is that Trump isn't fighting for democracy but for himself and his cronies. He wants the CIA to lie for him instead of his opponents and to help out the corporations who will back his reelection. Wouldn't it make more sense to have democratic control over all aspects of our lives, rather than leaving our fates either in the hands of a billionaire dictator ruling for his family and friends or an unelected "market" programmed to value profit over our well-being?

4

Why We Buy In

Until 2016, political consultants were widely seen as master manipulators, which never quite made sense to me. After all, if guys like Karl Rove and David Axelrod were such geniuses at propaganda, why could they never convince more than half of eligible voters to show up on Election Day? Despite (or perhaps because of) the effort that goes into focus groups, press releases, and speech writing, most Americans despise politicians. The main focus of any campaign is not to reverse this dynamic but to selectively enhance it, to kindle our fear and hatred of the opposition to the point that we'll come up with our own reasons to support their guy.

This is now obvious. Trump did everything wrong during his campaign. He insulted the family of a fallen soldier, fired two campaign managers, and was caught on tape bragging about being a sexual predator. He was wildly disliked, not just among "coastal elites" but everywhere. Here's a remarkable Associated Press report from April 2016:

> Seven in 10 people, including close to half of Republican voters, have an unfavorable view of Trump. . . . It's an opinion shared by majorities of men and women; young and old; conservatives,

moderates and liberals; and whites, Hispanics and blacks—a devastatingly broad indictment of the billionaire businessman.

Even in the South, a region where Trump has won GOP primaries decisively, close to 70 percent view him unfavorably. And among whites without a college education, one of Trump's most loyal voting blocs, 55 percent have a negative opinion.

And yet Trump managed to go on to win the presidency because, like an unskilled but dirty basketball team, he has a genius for bringing down everyone around him—opponents, reporters, debate moderators—to play the game at his grubby level. He knew he couldn't handle a one-on-one debate with Clinton, for example, so he pulled a move from his days on the Wrestlemania circuit and invited plants to sit in the front row and try to rattle her. First he brought in women who had accused Bill of being a sexual predator, and then he invited Obama's estranged half-brother, who presumably was supposed to sneak on stage when the moderator wasn't looking and hit Clinton with a chair. (By the way, Clinton also got to invite people to sit in the front row, and given the choice of literally thousands of sympathetic people who have been screwed over by Trump, she chose. . . . Republican billionaires Mark Cuban and Meg Whitman. Is it really a surprise that she didn't win? To put this in Muppet terms, no one wants to give Animal the nuclear codes, but he'd have a shot if his opponent were Sam the Eagle.)

Trump's campaign was the logical evolution of a political culture that was already almost entirely based on demonizing the opposing candidate. Long ago the American political class mastered the jujitsu of using the force of our dissatisfaction with the status quo against us by channeling it against one of the two status quo parties and thus in support of the other. It wasn't an ideal arrangement—I'm sure our politicians would prefer to be loved than to be grudgingly tolerated—but it maintained stability while the national wealth was vacuumed up by the 1 percent, and that was good enough. Each election, candidates would praise the courage and wisdom of the American people, but you could always feel the contempt they really had for us in the unbearably bad quality of most campaign materials—especially compared to corporate advertising. Now those people actually are evil geniuses. For a half minute they can make me actually consider going on a late-night Taco Bell run despite a lifetime of evidence from my taste buds and intestines that it's a terrible idea.

A typical political ad during campaign season is about as subtle as a First World War propaganda poster: twenty seconds of creepy music and grainy black-and-white footage of the opponent, followed by a montage of our smiling candidate in the bright sunshine with family, soldiers, dog, and the flag. If corporate ad guys made a spot like that, it'd be dripping in hipster self-awareness that might be annoying but would at least acknowledge our intelligence: *You know and we know that we are trying to sell you this Whopper, so let's have some fun with this relationship.*

By contrast, the analysis that goes into most campaign ads is astonishingly primitive. Here's how Democratic consultant Carter Eskew explained to the *New York Times* the conventional wisdom about the initial wave of general election commercials in 2012: "The first ads that are run are in many ways the most important because the mind is the most open and uncluttered at that point." Sigmund Freud created modern psychoanalysis over a hundred years ago and since that time I don't know that any professional outside the field of politics has described the human brain as an empty vessel just waiting to be filled. Jesus, maybe these guys actually thought *Vote Tom Barrett for Governor* was a brilliant sign.

We assume that campaign ads are effective because more money is spent on them each election. Could it be possible that we only think they work because the people who tout their supreme effectiveness are the campaign consultants paid to produce them and the media outlets paid to run them? As with most advertising, it's hard to generate definitive proof about the effectiveness of political spots, but here's one piece of anecdotal evidence: everybody hates them.

Imagine how much more fun campaign ads could be if they borrowed from the corporate world and adopted the classic strategy of marketing your weakness as your strength. In 2012 Mitt Romney could have embraced the criticism that he was an out-of-touch billionaire with a Polo-style ad featuring Mitt and a crew of gorgeous young blonde women and men on a yacht, frolicking in crisp white linen shirts and drinking gin and tonics. Obama could have countered with a "most interesting man in the world" campaign, featuring him in Indonesia laughing with imams, in Kenya dancing with the Masai, and at the Brandenburg Gate in Germany speaking to hundreds of thousands. The ads would have made us feel lucky that he had chosen our country to lead: "I don't often run for president, but when I do. . . ."

Trump had expert training in flaunting his weaknesses, since that's pretty much the job description of a reality television star. So Hillary needed to respond in kind. Instead of her doomed attempt at posing as a cuddly grandma, she and Bill should have bumped off Kevin Spacey, taken over the last season of *House of Cards*, and finally given us all a chance to get some enjoyment out of their ruthless scheming. It would have been worth it just for the episode where they dump Anthony Weiner's body in the woods.

As bad as they are at campaign ads, however, the two parties are masterful at the marketing strategy that's worked throughout American history: culture war. For parties with only minor policy disagreements facing a public that longs to feel like it has genuine options, it pays to play up their supposedly unbridgeable gaps in values and identities. Democrats are nice; Republicans are tough. Democrats like the underdog; Republicans appreciate success. Democrats like the Beatles; Republicans like Elvis. Most of us start identifying early on with one party or another through this virtual *Cosmo* quiz ("Are You a Red State or a Blue State?") that permeates the culture. Of course there are more substantial factors, such as which party passed labor and civil rights legislation, but the further these feats recede into ancient history the more they become points of identification rather than meaningful differences moving forward.

A major exception, of course, was Obama's campaign, which gave voters who supported civil rights a chance to actually advance them by electing an African American president. Republicans are still pissed because they think Obama got a free pass because he's Black, and you have to admit they have a point. History shows that it's been super easy for African Americans to become president of the United States.

By focusing on values, the parties allow themselves lots of wiggle room on policy. Bill Clinton was able to fulfill the long-standing Republican dream of ending welfare by framing it as the Democratic Party's compassionate way of helping the poor liberate themselves from government dependence, and Barack Obama managed to carry out more deportations than any president in history while somehow coming across as pro-immigrant. Republicans are especially good at turning policy debates into cultural crusades, portraying gun control laws and even the acknowledgment of climate change as alien invasions of elite liberal values into the American heartland. Now, Trump and his cabal of creeps like Jeff Sessions and Steve Bannon are pushing this deeper into the realm of open white nationalism.

The rise of cable news networks like Fox and MSNBC, catered to specific political niches, has dramatically increased the

perception that Republicans and Democrats occupy completely separate cultural worlds. And the ceaseless drive to keep their
viewers engaged and enraged leads them toward ever more shrill
caricatures, from the Republicans' open embrace of ignorance and
meanness on one station to the curdling of many Democrats into
condescending whiners on the other.

Negativity is the inevitable destination of a system in which
oligarchic parties constantly betray their voters, because our goals
become reduced to simply keeping the other party from winning.
And now that the powers of the executive branch have massively
expanded to include oversight of vast domestic surveillance networks and drone assassination lists, the stakes have only gotten
higher for activists to keep their party in power.

But for all their ugliness, elections also demand our attention
with their undeniable human drama. People complain that politics
has become a reality show, but that gets the chronology wrong.
Politics is the original, and by far the most gripping, reality show,
and modern democracy has opened up to the masses the stories
of palace intrigues that used to be reserved for aristocratic insiders. There is the comedy of watching a cutthroat competition of a
bunch of rich successful people who are obviously screwed up on
some deep emotional level that leads them to subject themselves
and everybody in their lives to this public inquisition. But the
heart of the story is driven by the personalities and the biographies
of the candidates, which the successful ones are able to somehow
sell to us as an embodiment of our own aspirations.

In 2008, Obama's achievement was, as Ron Suskind put it in
Confidence Men, his insider account of Obama's first two years in
office, to "weave his story into the broader story of the nation" and
to link in our minds his personal victory with America's continued
progress. By contrast, George W. Bush was the black sheep of a

wealthy establishment Republican family that was a world away from most Americans, but he remodeled his image as that of a self-made conservative outsider and connected with ordinary folks by tapping into the pain of his lifelong thinking problem. Bush had had the misfortune of attending Yale during the late 1960s, a brief moment when the Ivy League's historic mission was transitioning from aristocratic segregation to hedge fund preparation, and students were at least partially judged on their intelligence. The experience left Dubya with an enduring bitterness against the elitism of those who speak in full sentences.

Trump has built a similar unlikely connection with his followers. The son of a rich real estate developer from Queens, Trump spent his whole life trying to buy his way into Manhattan high society, only to find himself mocked for his buffoonery. That's why he is at war with the cultural elites but still seems perpetually unsatisfied because he can't win their approval. Here's Sidney Blumenthal's withering portrait in the *London Review of Books*:

> "We don't win anymore," Trump lamented. His reverent followers took his omnipotent image from his reality show as the reality and his anger as something felt on their behalf. They didn't understand his inner injury. Rousing the crowds at his rallies to a fever pitch—"knock the crap out of them"—he encouraged an atmosphere of violence and fear. Watching Trump incite his pitchfork revolt, New Yorkers were merely astounded that others couldn't recognize his all too familiar stuntmanship. He knew he had to cross the Hudson to find true believers, but the further into *Duck Dynasty* territory he ventured the more it felt like banishment to Queens.

These personal narratives are genuinely compelling, and the twists and turns of their daily competition on the campaign trail fill the daily programming of the news industry, which value-adds microscopic analysis to every trivial event and then telescopically analyzes the even more trivial impact of its own coverage. As with everything else in our lives, the result is that we spend more time watching things that we used to actually do. Cooking shows replace cooking, sports debate shows replace physical activity, and political shows replace activism and civic participation. If you really want to get involved in the election, the best you can do is respond to one of those urgent election-year emails to make a three-dollar donation, so that you can have the satisfaction of knowing that you played a part in putting another one of those goddamn ads on the air.

This reality show worked smoothly for many decades, taking the country on a wild ride every four years that would eventually and inevitably weed out the bad apples, through a lack of fundraising or media exposure or approval, and then safely return to one of the handful of establishment-approved candidates that we all could have predicted would win from the start. But in 2016, the rickety contraption went off the rails.

Years of mounting frustration with the government's inability to address growing inequality and dysfunction finally broke through—just as it has recently in Europe, where hard-right anti-immigrant parties have risen to ruling or leading-contender status in France, Hungary, and elsewhere, while strong new left-wing parties have emerged in Greece, Spain, and Portugal. In the United States this growing polarization between left and right was shoehorned into our two-party system, to the horror of the leaderships of both parties.

If I had to sum up the 2016 election in one sentence, it would be this: the Republican Party was too divided and discredited to stop Trump, the Democratic Party closed ranks to block Bernie Sanders, and, as a result, Trump was the only alternative in November to the hated Wall Street–funded status quo represented by Hillary Clinton. I do have more than one sentence, however, so let's dig into how we got to that explosive point.

The central story of mainstream US politics over the past few decades is the Republicans' steady evolution from the leading party of world capitalism to a semi-unhinged fringe that wants a prison state for Blacks and Latinxs, complete anarchy for corporations, and politicians who will pander to their every Internet conspiracy—while still commanding the resources and power befitting one of the two parties in a two-party system. This relentless rightward trajectory has been accelerated by the party's need to differentiate itself from a Democratic Party also moving rightward, as well as by its unmooring from its three main ideological strengths in recent years.

First, the ongoing disastrous consequences of the Iraq War, supported by most Democrats but infamously and incompetently led by George W. Bush, weakened the Republicans' reputation as the party of national security. Second, the global financial crisis and bank bailouts undermined the dogma of the free market—a belief system also shared by most Democrats but traditionally associated with the Republicans. Lastly, the incomplete but profound victories of the movement for LGBTQ equality, legally but especially culturally, have deprived the Republicans of one of their key culture wars in most of nonrural America.

So, while the party was able to dominate many states and regions—sometimes through dirty tricks like gerrymandering the boundaries of voting districts to give themselves better odds—on a national level it didn't have any coherent message other than "Things were better back in my day, dagnabbit!" In this vacuum, the party became a collection of loudmouths and lowlifes competing for the attention of a shrinking but passionate base of pure reaction, which has been fertile ground for con artists posing as candidates for a few months to soak the rubes. Sarah Palin, Newt Gingrich, and Herman Cain took full advantage of the Republican primaries to audition for Fox News and sell their books. Trump also, by many accounts, initially saw his presidential run as a simple exercise in brand building, but his timing was different.

By 2016 the party diehards had moved too far to the right to accept another Mitt Romney type, and the strain of pandering to them while simultaneously appealing to the general public was too much for early favorites like Jeb Bush and Marco Rubio, who came across like traumatized Ken dolls after years of rough play. Trump's "America First" nationalism was an echo of Pat Buchanan's Republican primary campaign in 1992. Like Buchanan, Trump had the support in the early primaries of roughly a third of the electorate. But the same number that left Buchanan a clear loser in a one-on-one race with George H. W. Bush was enough to win Trump many of the early states in a comically overcrowded 2016 Republican field.

Trump may not have been that popular among Republican voters, but the party leadership was liked even less. It's revealing that Trump only started winning more than 35 to 40 percent in state primaries when his opponents tried to unite against him and publicly floated ideas for blocking his nomination at the party convention. It was an elaborate plan that never factored in the part where voters were supposed to choose someone else, and it only succeeded in allowing Trump to claim that, once again, the elites were conspiring against him, and began the process of his winning majority support inside the party.

Meanwhile, the Democratic Party was being rocked by its own internal rebellion, as an aging Jewish self-described socialist—whose thick Brooklyn accent amusingly belied his "Senator from Vermont" label—came out of nowhere to seriously challenge what the entire country had assumed would be a year-long coronation of Hillary Clinton as the party's presidential nominee. Bernie Sanders's proposals for funding universal health care and college education through major tax increases on the rich reignited the fire of protest that, for almost two decades, has made explosive appearances every few years: the 1999 "Battle in Seattle" against the World Trade Organization; the enormous protests against the Iraq War in 2003 and anti-immigration legislation in 2006; and the Occupy and Black Lives Matter movements in the Obama years.

But these movements have for the most part been successfully defused by the Democrats' recurring message with every election that protesting is less important than entering the electoral arena to stop the latest threat of Republican apocalypse. Demands for amnesty for all immigrants and bringing all the troops home were dropped, Beltway talking points about bipartisan immigration reform and responsibly waging the fight against terror were raised. And so Democratic Party leaders were far more united and confident than their Republican counterparts about shoving an unpopular mainstream candidate down their voters' throats. After all, they figured, even if Hillary Clinton was an uninspiring candidate, the Republicans were in such disarray that they were about to nominate a candidate who couldn't possibly beat her in November.

Take a step back to look at the overall process, and you'll notice a striking result. The New Deal liberal program of Bernie Sanders was barred from the political system on the grounds that it was too extreme, but the door to the world's most powerful office was left wide open to an erratic racist whose semi-fascist advisors spoke excitedly about tearing down global capitalist institutions. As Dan O'Sullivan concluded in a post-election article for *Jacobin*, "Incredible though it may seem, our systems are better girded against a soft left than a hard right."

Donald Trump's election is the ultimate indictment of the American version of democracy because it disproves what is supposed to be our democracy's most basic virtue. We're told that our system of checks and balances, the Electoral College, and the rest may be inefficient and even borderline dysfunctional, but at least they work to promote stability and prevent despotism. Well, guess what? We now have an unstable despot, and it's because of this same vaunted system, which at every turn instinctively supports the few over the many and treats a rogue, racist billionaire as a harmless nuisance but sees danger in the raised expectations of tens of millions of working-class people that a better life is possible.

PART II

From Hope to Dope

5

Obama: The God That Failed

wo thousand sixteen was certainly a wild election year, but it's amazing how quickly we forget that there have been two other wild ones already in this century—perhaps because this is a country where every presidential election is called the "most important of our lifetime," and liberals and conservatives alike demand that you shut up and not mention that we were told the same thing four years earlier.

I realize there were no smartphones or hashtags in 2000, but is it that hard to remember that the presidency was stolen for George W. Bush? Roger Stone, now part of Trump's devious inner circle, organized a mob of hundreds of Republican staffers to barge into a Dade County office to intimidate election officers into postponing a recount that would have given the election to Al Gore. And in their outrageous *Bush v. Gore* ruling, the five Republican appointees on the Supreme Court upheld blocking the recount even as they admitted that their decision wasn't based on any precedent and that its logic was "limited to the present circumstances" and couldn't be used in any future decisions.

Then there's 2008, which started with Obama vs. Hillary in the

Democratic primaries, which was both a noble contest against historic barriers and a dirty knife fight between two win-at-all-costs brawlers. Obama was so determined to score a victory over racism that he was willing to flirt with sexism ("You're likeable enough, Hillary"), and Clinton was so eager to vanquish sexism that she resorted to racism ("Senator Obama's support among hard-working Americans, white Americans, is weakening"). Then, before Obama could even finish his victory lap over the summer, his Republican opponent, John McCain, tapped the previously unknown Sarah Palin into the ring, and all hell broke loose. Donald Trump's politics were coming out of a former beauty pageant contestant with the temperament of a rabid squirrel. This unleashed a very American combination of lust and moral righteousness among the Republican base—until Palin collapsed under the pressure of the easiest question in history (name a single newspaper or magazine that you've recently read) and Tina Fey's subsequent devastating impression on *Saturday Night Live*. The final outcome was never in doubt, but Election Night was historic nonetheless, with Obama celebrating in front of a quarter million people weeping with joy in Chicago's Grant Park.

But the strangest thing of all about 2008 was that it was an election that made people feel . . . good. Less than a decade later, it's easy to forget just how much Barack Obama inspired people and struck them as a completely unprecedented political figure—certainly in my lifetime—and not only because he was a Black man whose middle name was Hussein. He was an intellectual and a preacher capable of brilliant speeches that respected the intelligence and dignity of his listeners. He was also, eight years before Bernie Sanders, the first major candidate in recent memory to come out of the actual left.

Not the far left of Fox News fantasies, where radical feminists, Black Lives Matter organizers, and ISIS agents meet at secret campsites to swap bomb recipes and trade secrets on how to dupe the liberal media, or even the actual far left, whose prospects were way too dim for his personal ambitions, but Obama was once upon a time a genuine activist. He helped lead rallies against apartheid South Africa in college and spent time as a community organizer on the South Side of Chicago. When you read the passages in his memoir *Dreams from My Father* about the positive lessons he gained from working in coalitions with members of the Nation of Islam, you can see why his election to the presidency felt to people like Rush Limbaugh like the beginning of the End Times.

Once Obama decided to enter politics, he quickly adopted centrist policies, but he retained the leftist rhetoric about bottom-up change all the way through his presidential run. That was the meaning of "We are the change we have been waiting for" and certainly his campaign slogan "Yes we can," which is the English version of the protest chant made famous by Cesar Chavez and the movement of Chicano farmworkers, "¡Sí, se puede!" When conservatives complain that it's unfair to pigeonhole their Obama hatred as racist, they have a point. Their hatred is not only racist but also steeped in a general hostility to the themes of equality, justice, and humanity that Obama invoked. These fears about Obama's leftist militancy were pretty silly given the boatloads of donations he was receiving from Wall Street bankers, who presumably were assured that their investments would be safe no matter what he said in those beautiful speeches. For most Obama supporters, meanwhile, the attraction wasn't his distant past as a student activist but the more recent history of 2002 when, as a little-known state official in Illinois, he gave a speech against the Iraq War.

Iraq was the defining issue of the Bush years. A month before the war began, ten million people took to the streets of New York, London, Rome, Tokyo, Mexico City, Johannesburg, and hundreds of other cities, a stunning display that led *New York Times* reporter Patrick Tyler to famously write that "there may still be two super-powers on the planet: the United States and world public opinion." The February 15, 2003, global day of protest showed that across the planet, the sympathy and goodwill extended toward the United States after September 11 had rapidly curdled into disgust at the bullying smirks of its prep-school frat-boy president. Within the homeland, the situation was more polarized. Some folks loved preemptive war and "You're either with us or against us." Most people who voted Democratic hated it.

Rather than representing this sentiment in Congress, however, Democrats provided Bush with the necessary votes not merely to authorize the Iraq War but to do so with a strong majority. In 2004 Howard Dean galvanized Democratic voters with his stance against the Iraq War, but the party establishment took him out before the primaries even started. By 2008, however, with the war such a lost cause that even Bush had started pulling out troops, the Democrats were finally feeling brave enough to let the voters have their antiwar candidate. As we would get to know Obama over his eight years in the White House, a sad irony became clear: if he'd had any inkling in 2002 that he was so close to the presidency, he never would have risked making the speech that helped get him there.

In any case, Obama took office with an almost 80 percent approval rating—more support than any incoming president in modern memory—as well as the largest Democratic majority in the House of Representatives since 1992 and the largest majority in the Senate since 1977. Expectations were understandably sky-high: 72 percent of respondents told Gallup that they expected the country to be better off four years later. It took the new president less than two months to fail the decisive test of his presidency, begin to puncture the hopes of his supporters, and set in motion the backlash that is still unfolding.

By the time Obama took office, the key issue of the day was no longer Iraq—though that was (and is) still a mess—but a global financial crisis unlike anything since the Great Depression. In the fall of 2008 the financial system froze when Lehman Brothers collapsed in a pile of fraudulent debt and all the other banks had no idea how much of the pretend money that they traded back and forth each day was backed up by real money. Even if most of us couldn't keep up with all the technical economic terms, we could see the panic among people who don't usually panic. The normally glib covers of the *Economist* featured a whirlpool ("What's Next?"), a man looking over a cliff ("World on Edge"), the planet falling through space ("Saving the System"), and a predator felled by arrows ("Capitalism at Bay"). Only proper English decorum prevented the magazine from running a picture of stained pants and the headline "Soiling our Britches."

Leaders around the world, including Bush and Obama, responded with taxpayer-funded bailouts to rescue the banks from the mess created by their own criminal and negligent schemes. It was a defining moment that has continued to shape the radicalization of politics on both the right and left. For a few months millions of Americans asked each other a question normally unspoken in America: "What do these billionaires actually produce that's useful to society?" Polls reported that a major portion of the population preferred socialism to capitalism, especially young people, as Bernie Sanders would later decisively confirm.

In public, Obama seemed to get off to a decent start by pushing through an enormous economic stimulus package, which many at the time thought would be the beginning of many more aggressive government policies to come. It turned out instead that it was a March 2009 private meeting with the heads of the nation's largest banks that would prove to be his defining moment.

The massive public outrage at the government bailouts gave the president enormous leverage to impose major reforms on the banks' accounting rules, risky investment strategies, and bloated executive compensation. In *Confidence Men*, Ron Suskind describes what happened in the meeting. The bankers entered the White House "nervous in ways these men are never nervous." They had good reason to be scared. The government bailouts of the banks not only had infuriated the public but they also gave the president vast potential leverage to impose conditions on the banks' accounting rules, investment strategies, and—gasp—CEO compensation. Obama's position was further enhanced by his massive approval ratings, his party's control of both houses of Congress, and the overall climate of shock at the financial crisis—even many Republicans were saying that the government might have to take over many banks. Rarely has a president ever had so much leverage over the lords of finance. Then, according to Suskind, Obama laid his cards on the table:

> My administration is the only thing between you and the pitchforks. You guys have an acute public-relations problem that's turning into a political problem. And I want to help. But you need to show that you get that this is a crisis and that everyone has to make some sacrifices. I'm not out there to go after you. I'm protecting you. But if I'm going to shield you from public and congressional anger, you have to give me something to work with on these issues of compensation.

I want to help. . . . I'm protecting you. That's all the bankers needed to hear. Suskind reports that the bankers relaxed after Obama's dramatic speech and offered him few specific suggestions. The president had tried to scare them with hypothetical angry townspeople, but these guys had him nailed as soon as he made it clear that he wasn't there to represent his voters against them. The CEOs emerged from the meeting with their sense of entitlement fully restored. Soon they would be pushing back against even Obama's most limited reforms and berating him when he would dare to make even toothless complaints about their industry.

A pattern was set for the next eight years. Time and again, in the name of bipartisan compromise, Obama and the Democrats negotiated away their supporters' demands, only to watch their opponents come up with more extreme new positions. Their plans to address our obscene health care system started off by ruling out genuine universal health care (because a program that exists in every other developed nation is clearly unrealistic), then abandoned even a "public option" alternative to for-profit insurance companies, and finally ended up with a "universal" health-insurance law that was literally written by an insurance company executive. Even still, not a single Senate Republican voted for the Affordable Care Act.

Obama's failed attempt to reach an immigration deal was even more disastrous. In his first two years, Democrats had control of both houses of Congress but didn't pass any laws to reduce deportations or provide a path to legalization and citizenship. Even after the Republicans won Congress and blocked any chance at major legislation, Obama could have taken executive actions—the way Trump did as soon as he came into office—to pardon millions of undocumented immigrants or declare a moratorium on deportations. He could have even just threatened to take these kinds of actions in order to pressure Republicans in Congress to come to the table. Instead, he ramped up deportations to record levels to convince the Republicans that he was "serious about enforcement" and therefore they should be serious about legalization, which only succeeded in pushing the entire immigration debate rightward. To his outraged supporters, he claimed to not have legal authority to act without Congress—until immigrant students started protesting at his campaign offices as he was beginning his 2012 reelection campaign. At that point he made the discovery that he did in fact have the executive power to create the Deferred Action program, which gave hundreds of thousands of young immigrants temporary legal status.

While Obama's team regularly caved to Republicans, they were quite militant when it came to smacking down their own frustrated voters. When, in the months leading up to the midterm elections in 2010, progressives started to grumble about how few major accomplishments their party had made in the two years they held the presidency and both houses of Congress, the White House decided it was time for some straight talk about pragmatism.

"The idea that we've got a lack of enthusiasm in the Democratic base, that people are sitting on their hands complaining, is just irresponsible," Obama told *Rolling Stone*. "If people now want to take their ball and go home, that tells me folks weren't serious in the first place." Vice president Joe Biden similarly told supporters to "stop whining," and press secretary Robert Gibbs complained about the "professional left" that would only "be satisfied when we have Canadian health care, and we've eliminated the Pentagon." I have to admit that I am one of those people who like the sound of Gibbs's dystopian nightmare of world peace and free medicine. But it was odd to hear Obama's spokesman sound so much like Alex Jones in his description of people with the audacity to still hope for change.

The Obama team pitched their shitty compromises as savvy realism, but they actually made for a horrible electoral strategy that demoralized Democrats and only pushed Republicans to further reactionary extremes. Yet no matter how many times his opponents refused to take yes for an answer, Obama continued to push for his

beloved bipartisan consensus, a testament not to his noble ideal-
ism but his negligent narcissism. Like most successful politicians,
Obama took his electoral success as proof of his destiny to be the
one to overcome seemingly insurmountable national problems based
on the glorious force of his personality. And like many one-time
activists who long ago decided their time would be better spent
(and compensated) working for change "inside the system," Obama
overestimated his ability to negotiate concessions from the rich and
powerful. He confused his own willingness to reconcile his internal
conflict between ideals and ambition with his chances of reconcil-
ing the far more intractable conflicts between people losing their
homes and the banks that were taking them. The result was that the
president who came into office with the highest expectations in recent history ended up with a slim list of recognizable achievements:
an unpopular health insurance program, temporary (and reversible)
protection for some young immigrants, and the claim that without
him the economy and the Middle East would be even worse.

During the reelection campaign in 2012, the Obama campaign floated the slogan: "Bin Laden is dead and GM is alive."
On paper it sounded like a winner, a nice spin on the administration's foreign and domestic accomplishments. But the slogan
inadvertently captured more of what we've lost in the Obama era
than what we've won. The assassination of Osama bin Laden was
carried out in Pakistan by Navy SEALs, a result of Obama's shift
from massive military occupations to covert operations in countries with which we're not even at war. The rebirth of General
Motors was the result of a government bailout and bankruptcy
restructuring that eviscerated union contracts and cut workers' pay
in half. No wonder the campaign slogan never took off: it was a
salute to the expansion of military lawlessness from the Bush years
and the final deathblow to the blue-collar American Dream. That's

not the way most Democratic voters would have put it, but in their bones they knew that the killing of bin Laden hadn't halted the perpetual War on Terror and the saving of GM hadn't brought back the path to a comfortable life that the auto industry had once represented to millions of workers. Fear of the next Osama bin Laden is very much alive, while the hope that General Motors used to represent is dead and gone.

Ironically, Obama's helplessness and passivity with corporations and police departments eventually led to the emergence of the types of protest movements he had eloquently praised in his "Yes we can" days as a candidate. Through his own negative example, Obama helped show an entire generation that the corruption and incompetence of our government is systemic and not personal. The impact of this realization played a role in the emergence of the Occupy movement and the Movement for Black Lives. But for every person who was radicalized by the Obama years, ten more were disillusioned and demobilized. Antiwar protests disappeared, immigrant marches dwindled, and dreams gradually faded, even as people continued to be solidly in Obama's corner—after all, his presidency was still historic. But Trump's presidency is historic as well, and Trump is using the magnitude of his moment, albeit incompetently, to try to enact massive immediate change. By contrast, Obama used his immense momentum to stall his supporters for as long as possible. He was an inspirational teacher for an entire generation, but instead of "Seize the day!" his message was "Lower your sights!" and "Accept that change is incremental!"

And so many of the people who put their trust in Barack Obama simply watched him and waited. They watched him get pushed around by bankers who wouldn't have jobs without government bailouts and Republicans who didn't have the votes in his first two years to stop anything the Democrats could have proposed in Congress. They watched their neighbors fall behind on their mortgages and their kids rack up student debt, and they waited. They wanted Obama to succeed so badly, this man who broke barriers and spoke with unparalleled intelligence and feeling. They wanted him to prove that the American Dream still can work—for him and for us. So they said, "Give him more time," and "We can't expect him to change everything at once." And then they watched Republicans rebuild their party under Obama's nose, watched them launch a Tea Party whose slogans made no sense but whose populist anger sure did. And they watched these rebranded Republicans take over Congress and vow to reverse all of Obama's radical laws, by which they really meant (since Obama hadn't actually done that much) most government programs created over the past century. And then they watched an even more sinister wing take form around the vilest figure of them all: the reality show host who got into politics by claiming that the first Black president was actually a foreigner and secret Muslim.

It was inevitable that having an African American president of a country with racism embedded in its founding DNA was going to strike some people as an intense waking nightmare that called into question everything they thought they understood about the world. For some, the sight of an attractive African American family frolicking on the White House lawn was the first step in the coming apocalypse that would culminate in a Manifest Undestiny of Mexicans and Native peoples rising up and driving whites to the sea. This paranoia fueled the Tea Party, which waved the Constitution at the Black President the way one would shake garlic at a vampire. It wasn't the content of the Constitution that appealed to these folks—as would become obvious when they went for Trump as dictator-in-waiting—but its symbolism as a relic from a time when men were men, youth had respect, and Black people were meant to build the White House, not live in it.

Republican leaders dabbled in anti-Obama racism from the start, from Sarah Palin's line in 2008 that he isn't "one of us" to Romney supporter John Sununu's comment in 2012 that Obama needed to "learn how to be an American." Some candidates went boldly into more openly racist waters that year. Before the South Carolina primary, Newt Gingrich called Obama the "food stamp president" and then smirkingly denied that the line had any racial connotations and was instead a mere statement of fact that more Americans had been receiving food stamps (as if it's a bad thing for a government program to prevent malnutrition). A few weeks earlier, Rick Santorum had described welfare to Iowa voters as an attempt to "make black people's lives better by giving them somebody else's money." Santorum later tried to claim that he had actually said "blah people's lives." This was potentially a very interesting lie, and I was hoping that Santorum would go on to elaborate a grand theory that those on welfare miss out on capitalism's excitement and become just sort of "blah." But few politicians have such a Gingrichian confidence in their ability to bullshit an entire country.

Beyond the official statements of politicians were the countless racist remarks from local Republicans that went viral every few months. A Puerto Rican conservative consultant named Heidi Wys was apparently so enraged at Obama's announcement of his wife's upcoming birthday that she tweeted, "Take her to Burger King, buy her a sundae with double banana, take her to your homeland, Kenya!" Wys followed up by tweeting, "I am not racist. My favorite nieces are dark-skinned! I'm Anti-Obama." Beyond Wys's random dis of her white nieces, her defense was almost identical to that of Richard Cebull, the chief district judge in Montana, after he was caught sending a nasty joke about Obama's mother to some buddies: "I didn't send it as racist, although that's what it is. I sent it out because it's anti-Obama." Just so we're clear about where Wys and Cebull were coming from: They're not racist. They just happen to hate Obama so much (not because he's Black) that they're willing to say racist stuff (which normally they would never do) because he just happens to be Black and they hate Obama (not because he's Black) even more than they hate racism.

Sadly, these sporadic outbursts seem almost quaint compared to the explosion of hate crimes and harassment against Muslims, Latinxs, African Americans, and Jews that began during Trump's campaign and have continued into his presidency. As we descend deeper into the Terrordome of the forty-fifth president, the stature of his predecessor will probably only increase. But if we are going to fondly remember the hopes that Obama once inspired, we should understand that it was the failure to deliver on those hopes that has ushered in an era of cynicism well suited for a lifelong real-estate hustler and self-branding specialist. As most people's living standards stagnated or declined after the Great Recession while the rich quickly recovered and inequality skyrocketed, some people turned away from Obama and toward Trump. Many more still liked Obama but concluded that if even he couldn't deliver hope and change, then there is no hope.

The fact that Obama's greatest personal strengths—dignity and intelligence—were used to further entrench the power of thoroughly corrupt institutions from the Pentagon to Wall Street should tell us that the change we have been waiting for isn't going to happen through a mere personnel switch in the Oval Office.

6

Trump, Patriotism, and Self-Loathing

Now we have a president whose message is that there is no noble American struggle in which we all take part. The universal *we* of "Yes we can" has been replaced. There is only *us* and *them*—Mexicans, Muslims, criminals, terrorists—in a world that's just a series of deals, with winners and losers, and all that happy talk about "Yes we can" will only blind you to the *them* who are trying to take what's rightfully yours. Trump's "America First" rhetoric shocks many who know its origins as a 1930s slogan of fascist sympathizers, but, unfortunately, it sounds perfectly logical to many others raised in a land where both liberals and conservatives pledge allegiance to that inherently blind and stupid sentiment called *patriotism*.

It's fine to appreciate the good things about our country and celebrate the heroes, from Harriet Tubman to Rosa Parks, who have actually fought to defend our freedoms. What doesn't make sense is to assume that our country is better than others just because we live in it, much less to value the lives of those who live inside its borders over those who don't. But this is a minority view. Polls consistently show that most Americans think their country either "stands above all other countries" or is "one of the greatest countries" in the world. Really? There are literally hundreds of other countries out there, many of which have really cool things that we don't, like kangaroos, pyramids, thousand-year-old traditions of epic poetry, and universal health care. Most of us know nothing about these things, because few of us have the money or time off to travel, which in itself probably should knock this country out of "World's Greatest" medal consideration.

Like Pangloss, the relentless philosopher of optimism in Voltaire's *Candide*, who asserts in the face of untold destruction and misery that this is "the best of all possible worlds" because it is the one God created, until recently most Americans were determined to believe that we live in the best of all possible countries—despite mounting evidence to the contrary. According to an internal Pentagon study of nine military operations since the September 11, 2001, attacks, the US record is zero wins, two losses, and seven ties.* That's the record of a last-place soccer team—sorry, I should be more patriotic; make that a last-place NFL team. But somehow, fighting nine wars without a single victory doesn't make anyone question the whole "greatest fighting force the world has ever seen" thing. If someone told you that the US men's soccer team was the best in the world despite the results of every World Cup, you'd think they were delusional. Multiply that by 300 million people, apply it to something a thousand times more important, and it's called *patriotism*.

We get a red, white, and blue booster shot every four years via the presidential election, which invariably features a "Who Loves America More?" sub-competition. There was a funny moment in

* The study was obtained by journalist Nick Turse. Look up his story "Win, Lose, or Draw" at the excellent TomDispatch.com.

2012, when Romney accused Obama of "declinism"—the outrageous belief that the United States isn't going to singlehandedly dominate the world forever. By contrast, Romney proudly proclaimed that we're heading for another "American Century," a phrase coined by *Time* magazine's publisher, Henry Luce, to describe the period of historic US hegemony after every other world power had been invaded or bombed to pieces in World War II. If Vegas were laying odds on the phrase historians will eventually give to the coming hundred years, "American Century" would come in behind not only "Chinese Century" but also "Brazilian Century" and even "Bridezilla Century," while sneaking in just ahead of "Good God! Look at That Giant Asteroid Coming Right . . ." (In case you're wondering, yes, of course Obama caved and soon made his own "American Century" speech.)

Donald Trump takes a backseat to no one when it comes to patriotic kitsch. The *New York Times* reports that his National Security Council staffers go into meetings with foreign counterparts carrying "Make America Great Again" coffee mugs. (No word yet on whether their pencils are inscribed with that old office chestnut, "You don't have to be crazy to work here. But it helps!") But Trump's patriotism is way darker than typical politicians' sunny clichés about God, freedom, and plucky small business owners. This is a guy who spends much of his free time bitterly commenting in the dark about his coverage on cable news shows, and who brags to people he barely knows that the best thing about celebrity is being able to get away with sexual assault.

So it shouldn't be surprising that when Trump wants to fire up a crowd about the U. S. of A., he talks not of "America the Beautiful" but a forlorn place where "attacks on our police, and the terrorism in our cities, threaten our very way of life," and whose borders are little more than velvet ropes where rapists and murderers exchange fist bumps on their way in to commit unspeakable "carnage" and "atrocities." Trump tells his audience about looking down from Air Force One at the landmass between Trump Tower and Mar-a-Lago and seeing a desolate plain of "rusted-out factories scattered like tombstones across the landscape." Throughout his campaign, pundits kept expecting Trump's bleak themes to eventually backfire, because they were sure that the American people wanted to hear something more positive. But what people wanted to hear was reality—they liked hearing Bernie Sanders declare that countries like Denmark have better social welfare policies than the United States and they liked hearing Trump acknowledge underreported catastrophes like factory closures and the opioid addiction epidemic.

Of course, the way Trump talks about these issues is not reality based. He blames the opioid crisis on Mexico instead of pill-pushing pharmaceutical companies and says nothing about the thousands of factories that are open but ban unions and pay a sub-living wage for backbreaking work. And he relies heavily on recycling the racist campfire stories that rattle around the echo chamber of Fox News and *Breitbart: Did you hear the one about how immigration in Europe has gotten so bad that entire cities have become "no-go zones" for the police? No, but did you know that Black neighborhoods in the United States are so rough that "you buy a loaf of bread and end up getting shot"?* These boogeyman tales are corny and sound like the frightened ramblings of an old man, which, of course, they are.

But Trump is much more skillful—and therefore dangerous— when he talks, as he did in his inauguration speech, about the wounded pride of an empire in decline and his rage and resentment toward the leaders who he believes have let it happen:

> For too long, a small group in our nation's capital has reaped the rewards of government while the people have borne the cost.

Washington flourished—but the people did not share in its wealth. Politicians prospered—but the jobs left, and the factories closed. The establishment protected itself, but not the citizens of our country. Their victories have not been your victories; their triumphs have not been your triumphs; and while they celebrated in our nation's capital, there was little to celebrate for struggling families all across our land. . . .

We assembled here today are issuing a new decree to be heard in every city, in every foreign capital, and in every hall of power. From this day forward, a new vision will govern our land. From this moment on, it's going to be America First.

This isn't a wild tale about marauding bands of immigrant-terror-thugs. It's an accusation that we've been sold out by our own country's ruling class that rings true because it is: we've been double-crossed for decades by people who told us to please rise for the national anthem while they raided our pension funds and stashed their wealth in overseas tax havens. Socialists look at this and conclude that nationalism is a con. The hard-right response is to double down on patriotism by accusing elites of treasonous collusion with their global counterparts against the good and decent folk in the homeland. The charge isn't just that they haven't protected us economically but also physically—from criminals, terrorists, drug dealers, and other forces of (ahem) darkness. "The most basic duty of government is to defend the lives of its own citizens," Trump declared at the Republican National Convention. "Any government that fails to do so is a government unworthy to lead."

Why wouldn't leaders defend our lives from obvious bad guys? Maybe all that political correctness is to keep people from uncovering a sinister elite plot. Antisemitism has made a stunning comeback under Trump because Jews have always played the role of treasonous villain in reactionary fantasies. But in the second decade of the twenty-first century, all conspiracy theories inevitably lead to Barack Hussein Obama. "Look, we're led by a man that either is not tough, not smart, or he's got something else in mind," Trump said after the massacre at Pulse, a gay club in Orlando. "He doesn't get it or he gets it better than anybody understands—it's one or the other and either one is unacceptable." Obama "birtherism" didn't just launch Trump's political career. Its themes fundamentally shaped the message that he projects as president, and it's infected the entire Republican Party.

Trump's blatantly self-interested nationalism poses a serious challenge to the longstanding American tradition of proclaiming itself as the world's leading force for upholding a global system of peace and order. More than any president in at least eighty years, he disregards the infrastructure of global institutions like the United Nations, NATO, and the European Union that the United States has carefully constructed to make itself the first country among supposed equals. Trump instead brings to the White House his narrow real-estate-developer worldview that reduces every global issue to one question: Are we winning or losing this deal? By rejecting the idea that the United States is committed to global institutions or their supposed ideals of global democracy and cooperation, Trump infuriates the foreign policy establishment—not because deep down they believe in all that stuff either, but because they understand that Trump is throwing away the "soft power" that has been a key component of America's global success. After Trump disparaged NATO, an aghast former State Department official told the *New York Times* that his comments were "a direct assault on the liberal order we've built since 1945 and a repudiation of the idea that the United States should lead the West. . . . NATO is the great power differential between the US and Russia, as our Asian alliances are the power differential between us and China."

But Trump is also on to something. Now that the United States has a global economic rival in China and major regional rivals on every continent, it isn't getting the bang for the buck that it used to from these global ideals and institutions, so why shouldn't we go it alone and try to get the best deal for ourselves like everyone else does? Ironically, the boastful "Make America Great Again" blowhard is the first president to acknowledge, even if unconsciously, that the United States is no longer the "indispensable nation" but part of a truly multipolar world. Trump is following a global nationalist trend. The worldwide recession of 2008 has discredited globalist economic policies in many countries and given rise both to radical new parties and leaders on both the left and (more often) the right. But it's still shocking to see this change happen in the world's largest economy—and the one that has gained the most (at least in some neighborhoods) from those policies.

Trump appeals to people's loss of faith not just in global institutions but also in American democracy. Sanders called our political system "rigged" as part of his call for strict limits on political donations and for a larger redistribution of wealth to get the rich to help pay for public health care and education. Trump calls it "rigged" to give himself a future excuse for any time he loses and to make the case for why it's okay if he rigs it some more for himself and his supporters. A big part of Trump's success as a politician comes from the fact that he acknowledges corruption—revels in it, actually—and promises his supporters that finally they can have a "real leader" working for them, instead of Goldman Sachs. (Yes, I wrote that sentence before he had hired half of Goldman to be in his cabinet.) The result is that someone who can't speak in public for five minutes without spouting an obvious untruth comes across to many as the only authentic guy in politics. He's obviously a part of the 1 percent, but he's positioned himself—and somehow his cabinet full of billionaires, too—as the leader of a rebellion against it, whose solution to our broken democracy is to break it even further and for us to let him be our dictator.

And what an enormous machinery of repression Trump has inherited from his liberal predecessor: a network of prisons and immigrant detention centers, the largest military in the world, and history's most extensive network of foreign and domestic surveillance. It was Obama who used his reputation as a thoughtful progressive to normalize War on Terror policies that many of his voters abhorred under George W. Bush. When the government's mass surveillance activities were exposed by the whistleblower Edward Snowden, Obama soothed Democratic voters with the knowledge that someone responsible would be in charge of this sensitive information. "In the abstract you can complain about Big Brother and how this is a potential program run amok," he said, "but when you actually look at the details, I think we've struck the right balance." Never mind that ordinary citizens were never granted access to "actually look at the details"—does anyone actually think that Trump will even pretend to give a damn about "balance"?

After winning the presidency based on an antiwar reputation, Obama also legitimated a Bush administration idea that once seemed outrageous: that we are to be locked in a permanent state of war. "For eight years that I've been in office," Obama said, in one of his final speeches before leaving office, "there has not been a day when a terrorist organization or some radicalized individual was not plotting to kill Americans. . . . I will become the first president of the United States to serve two full terms during a time of war." Obama scaled down the deployment of large numbers of troops, but he also greatly expanded the use of drones, cyberwar, and special operations forces—who are now active in 138 countries, more than twice as many nations as when he took office.* So don't worry about whether Trump is going to start a war. He's already in charge of a few dozen.

Even the darkest aspects of Trump's style, his authoritarianism and calls for a powerful leader in troubled times that seem to come right out of a Marvel comic, have strong preexisting roots in American politics—not in some distant past but right up to today. Even the most "optimistic" and smiley, seemingly un-Trumpian politician will routinely turn around and talk about how the country is in grave peril because "Washington" is broken. Politicians are only too happy to join us in blaming themselves (okay, other politicians) for failing us, which seems noble of them until you realize they're just trying to divert our attention from the folks who actually drove this country off a cliff but also fund their campaigns. This is a major role of the political class in a capitalist democracy. Remember Obama's words to the bankers, "My administration is the only thing between you and the pitchforks." Even the president knows that when there is genuine danger, his job is to take the bullet for the real leaders of the free world.

In fact, all the talk about broken government can be quite useful for further eroding the democracy that we still have. Consider the issue that's hovered in the background of politics for at least two decades: how to go about the gradual dismantling of Social Security and Medicare. Politicians in both parties want to avoid being attacked for going after two of the most popular and effective government programs in American history, but they also repeatedly declare that current funding for Social Security and Medicare is "unsustainable"—at least if we want to continue two

---

* This information is also brought to you by Nick Turse and TomDispatch.com (I told you it's a good site.) The article is called "The Year of the Commando."

of the most ineffective and immoral programs in American history: astronomical military spending and tax breaks for corporations.

In 2010 Obama turned to the most benign-sounding of completely undemocratic solutions: the bipartisan commission headed by safely retired politicians. The National Commission on Fiscal Responsibility and Reform, chaired by Republican Alan Simpson and Democrat Erskine Bowles, somehow came up with a plan to reduce funding for Social Security and Medicare *and* cut taxes for the wealthy and corporations. It's a bit odd for a committee supposedly devoted to finding ways of increasing government revenue to call for lowering taxes. Presumably, if Bowles and Simpson served on a task force to reduce childhood obesity their main recommendation would be to abolish all taxes on millionaires, who could then donate used Shake Weights to needy schools. The Simpson-Bowles report hasn't had a major impact yet but it still might turn out to be a template for future "bipartisan reforms."

Back when Obama created the fiscal commission, he said its job was to make "tough choices necessary to solve our fiscal problems." "Tough choices" is Washington-speak for things that party leaders and their financial backers have decided need to happen despite the democratic will of voters. This mistrust of the populace goes back to the country's earliest days, when many states blocked not only women and Blacks from voting but also white men who didn't own property, under the theory that only those with something at stake in society (which apparently doesn't include the health and wellbeing of you and your loved ones) could be trusted with the responsibility of having a vote. Voting rights have, of course, been expanded since then, but the basic capitalist value system that equates property ownership with responsibility persists. Thus, Obama began crafting the health care bill by convening a high-profile meeting of those he termed health care "stakeholders," by which he meant representatives of hospitals, doctors, insurance and pharmaceutical companies, and even a few unions, but no patient groups. Apparently, all of us who have mortal bodies are not stakeholders in what type of health care we will receive. If you really cared about it that much, you should have owned a hospital.

During the discussions about Social Security and Medicare, the conventional wisdom of television pundits with $200 haircuts is that most voters want to reduce the deficit and keep funding these two programs but are too dim to realize that they can't do both. Most of us watching don't take offense because we assume the pundit isn't calling us idiots, just most Americans. After all, if most of us weren't idiots, we wouldn't elect so many awful people as our leaders, right? The seeming populism of antipolitician rhetoric is often a nice cover for a nasty elitism toward the masses who vote for them.

In *Candide,* Pangloss is comically absurd because Voltaire is mocking the self-serving monarchist and religious dogma of his day that whatever happens is God's will. Today the old idea of the will of God has been rebooted as the law of the market: whatever crap we are served for food, entertainment, or political representation must be a reflection of our own demand. (You apparently overslept that morning we all had a rally demanding tasteless cloned tomatoes and the *Entourage* movie.) The logic of this argument, that they wouldn't make it if we didn't want it, is pretty flimsy when you consider the existence of an enormous advertising industry charged with getting us to want the stuff they've already decided to make. But it's even weaker when applied to American politics, a two party cartel that bars the entrepreneurial competition of third parties as dangerous extremism.

The successes of both Trump and Sanders show that our Panglossian view is fading. For many decades we accepted our political process as the fullest expression of democracy, and therefore had no one to blame but ourselves (okay, everyone else) for the results, and elections ironically came to be our regular demonstration to ourselves that we are unfit for self-rule. This steady erosion of our faith in our own democratic abilities is what paved the way for Trump, and his victory has forced many of us to realize that we live in a banana republic like everyone else. So let's start respecting this best of all possible countries a little less, and ourselves and one another a little more.

7

Nobody's Coming to Save Us

onald Trump isn't just the first president to come out of reality television. He's also our first conspiracy theory president. (The wait continues for America's first porn-star president, but it probably won't be long.) He built his political career spreading birther lies, and he's gone on to add so many more. During the campaign he wondered aloud if Supreme Court Justice Antonin Scalia had been murdered and implied that Ted Cruz's father was involved in the JFK assassination. Since taking office he's hinted that a wave of vandalism at Jewish cemeteries might be a false-flag operation to make him look bad and—oh my god, I just found out that, as I was writing the previous sentences, Trump was tweeting that Obama had secretly wiretapped him last year. I'm surprised we haven't heard him declare that "many people are saying" it can't be a coincidence that Hillary Clinton's 1969 college graduation speech at Wellesley just happened to be a mere two months before NASA staged the moon landing—I mean, wake up, sheeple!

Honestly, though, as Trump got ever closer to the presidency, most of us found ourselves using the conspiratorial *they,* as in "Are *they* really going to let this clown become the most powerful person in the world?" It's not a completely irrational question. Let's face it, there really is a *they*—not a secret society of Freemasons or a cabal of bankers but a very visible ruling class of business, political, military, and cultural leaders. We can quibble over the size of this class, depending on how broadly we want to define them, but their power over the rest of us is not up for debate. If you grew up in this country during the long period of its global dominance, you may not have liked this ruling class but you assumed *they* were firmly in control—although you might not have been aware of this assumption until Trump won, and you suddenly discovered what it felt like not to have it.

The omnipotence of the US ruling class has always been more a well-cultivated illusion than an iron law, and even that illusion had been fading long before the 2016 election. In this young century, *they* have overseen a catastrophic military defeat in Iraq and a crooked banking crisis that almost brought down the world financial system, all while proving incapable of stopping the fossil fuel emissions that threaten the viability of all human life in a few generations. So, while many of *them* despise Trump as a semifunctional egomaniac who threatens everything they hold dear, I also imagine that *they* resent him for being an unflattering mirror of *their* own failures and a caricature of *their* own greed, vanity, and power-lust.

It's frightening to have Trump holding the most powerful office in the world, especially when it comes to national security. But if we take a moment to consider the truly disastrous decisions that have been made in that arena by *them* since the turn of this century . . . well we certainly won't feel better, but at least we'll realize that our fates have been in horrible hands for a very long time.

The 2001 attacks on the World Trade Center and Pentagon did not have to lead to a generation-long war that has destroyed much of the Middle East, created the worst refugee crisis since World War II, and inspired waves of right-wing Muslim and anti-Muslim hate groups around the world. In theory, September 11 could just as easily have led to some deep reflection in ruling circles about why the CIA had organized and trained al-Qaeda in the first place and to perhaps reconsider the geopolitical impulses that led them to make such a bad decision. We forget this now but that process started to happen among ordinary people in the initial days after the attacks. A mile north of the fallen towers in Lower Manhattan, Union Square became a twenty-four-hour gathering spot for strangers to cry and sing. They had debates with one another about the appropriate political response to such an atrocity, and they famously asked a question that is very American in its genuine naivety: *Why do they hate us?*

It only took a few weeks for that question to be buried under a pile of war preparation and daily (false) bomb scares, and a few more weeks for the question itself to become downright suspicious: *They hate our freedoms. Who's asking?* And thus was born the War on Terror, a campaign to show the Islamic world how a civilized nation goes about using airplanes to kill people. Evildoers were confidently warned that America's leaders were prepared to fight (well, send others to fight) for generations. Inspiring prose was written about how the attacks were going to give Americans a new sense of united purpose. America looked forward to a decade of benevolent ass-whooping: Afghanistan and Iraq. Then Syria and Iran. Maybe France.

Instead, ten years later, America appeared to the world like a ragged mad king from the end of a Shakespearean tragedy: arrogant yet bewildered at what had gone wrong, still covered in the blood of Fallujah and Kandahar, instinctively firing off drones to new lands even as the economic realm lay in ruins. Adding to the theatricality of the moment, the country was ravaged by hurricanes and droughts, wildfires and tornadoes. Just before the ten-year anniversary of September 11, Washington and New York were again attacked, this time by Hurricane Irene, which submerged entire towns across the Northeast. Before that were the record heat waves, which themselves had come after an epic blizzard the previous winter. Now the question had become: *Why does the weather hate us?* Shakespeare might have attributed these disasters to divine retribution. Republican Michelle Bachmann said the same thing,* which proves that the difference between a genius and an idiot is about four hundred years.

If there was a cosmic message at work, the messenger was not God but Mother Nature. September 11 was used to wage war on the Muslim world because it happens to sit on top of the planet's largest reserves of oil and gas, which are known for a few things: they heat up the atmosphere, they are key strategic resources, and they make boatloads of money for a few people. You might think the first point is most important and that therefore we should plan a future without fossil fuels. Which is why you're not qualified to be a member of the American ruling class. For corporations, making money is always the top priority, and for the state, controlling the supply of fossil fuels coming out of the Middle East is a key check on expanding rivals like China. And so even as Obama replaced Bush, the wars continued in even more countries, the drilling expanded into fracking and tar sands, and in the fall of 2011 Americans found themselves running in fear from wildfires and floods, but simultaneously breathing a sigh of relief that the anniversary of September 11 had come and gone without any "terror."

....

* Exact quote from the then Congresswoman and presidential candidate: "I don't know how much God has to do to get the attention of the politicians. We've had an earthquake; we've had a hurricane."

This is the wild irrationality that's been in power since long before Trump took office. It comes from the fundamentally antihuman needs of our two most powerful institutions, business and government. In many ways, our democracy can be defined as the process by which we are taught to internalize those needs. Some believe that the rich and powerful should naturally be our leaders because they must have gotten to their positions by being smart. Even those of us who don't share that view often comfort ourselves with the thought that *they* hopefully won't screw things up too badly, since they have more of an interest than anybody in preserving a world that works best for them. It's an unconscious variation on the reactionary "stakeholder" idea that those who have the most skin in the game are the most qualified to run it. Karl Marx and Friedrich Engels flipped this theory on its head in the *Communist Manifesto* when they declared that, in an unjust society, the leaders should be the ones who have "nothing to lose but their chains."

Liberals and conservatives are divided over whether business or government should have ultimate authority—as if the two aren't completely intertwined through shared interests and the thousands of people whose careers shuttle back and forth between the two institutions. Lobbyists become regulators. Senators become senior partners. Tommy Franks, the army general who famously dismissed Iraqi casualties with the line "We don't do body counts," retired from the military and joined the board of Bank of America in 2005. Franks's no-counting philosophy apparently had a real institutional impact because within four years the bank had lost billions, and Tommy and the rest of the board were forced to step down. The story has a happy ending, however, as most banker stories do. Bank of America got $25 billion in bailouts and Tommy joined the board of a far more respected firm, Chuck E. Cheese.

In the months leading up to the election, most economists agreed that in the unlikely event of a Trump victory, all hell was going to break loose. After all, investors value stability and predictability, which would be in short supply with a tantrum-prone man-child in office. Financial markets rose and fell with Clinton's poll numbers. The *Economist*'s Intelligence Unit even listed Trump's winning the election as one of its top ten threats to the global economy—the first time the result of a US election had made the list. The near universal consensus that a Trump victory would crash the markets continued right up until he won and sent the markets soaring to record new heights over the coming months. The reason wasn't that Trump was any less incompetent and unpredictable than people had feared. It was that, once again, everybody had mistakenly assumed that rich people give a rat's ass about anything other than the prospect of corporate tax cuts.

Capitalists are very strange compared to other ruling classes throughout human history. For thousands of years, the same people who directed the labor of peasants, small farmers, and slaves were also in charge of their religion, education, and protection. They didn't divide their worldview between two separate spheres called *the economy* and *politics*. But today the most important decisions in our lives—whether to build a factory in our town, dump pollutants in our river, pay taxes into our school system—are made by a class that doesn't believe it has a responsibility to anyone but itself and its investors. A few of them might consider how these decisions impact their workers, consumers, and neighbors, but they're under no societal obligation to do so—that's a separate job for those losers in the government. Capitalists aren't necessarily better or worse human beings than previous ruling classes, but this radical individualism would have been bizarre to even the most tyrannical warlords and slave owners of the past. They exhibit extreme antisocial behavior that, if it weren't in the service of profit, would probably be seen as symptomatic of personality disorders. And nobody exhibits these disorders more clearly and proudly than Trump.

It's become an Internet hobby to give Trump a psychiatric diagnosis as a way to discredit or demean him, which is childish and only further stigmatizes the millions of people who will suffer immensely if Trump is able to pass his planned drastic cuts to mental health care. But we can recognize that he has clear and severe emotional limitations. He doesn't register joy or sorrow, only victory and defeat. He can't smile, only smirk. I have no idea how a psychiatrist would diagnose Trump, and I don't care. What's more important is he's a symptom of a societal disease, a system that rewards, promotes, and develops our most antihuman traits.

Back in 2011, the *Journal of Business Ethics* published a paper by British academic Clive R. Boddy titled, "The Corporate Psychopaths Theory of the Global Financial Crisis," which, according to its abstract, is

> A very short theoretical paper but is one that may be very important to the future of capitalism because it discusses significant ways in which Corporate Psychopaths may have acted recently, to the detriment of many. Further research into this theory is called for.

Hear, hear and quite so, Professor Boddy. I hereby join your call for further enquiry into this matter of corporate psychopaths—as well as any and all possible roles played in our recent financial troubles by zombies, vampires, and demonic clowns. Peer-reviewed journals generally don't engage in this sort of name-calling. *European History Quarterly* doesn't run articles with titles like "The 'Russians Are Just Asswipes' Theory of the Origins of the Crimean

War." But the specter of the Wall Street sociopath has been an increasing topic of scholarly discussion since at least the early 2000s, when business giants Enron and WorldCom went bankrupt in a heap of debt and fraud. That caught the attention of psychiatrist Robert Hare, creator of the "Psychopath Checklist."

Hare had worked for decades in the field of criminology, where his handy listicle for the human psyche was quite popular among parole board members who hated spending more than a few precious minutes deciding where incarcerated people were going to spend their next three to five years. By 2002 he had come to focus on the big-time criminals: the executives at Enron and WorldCom, he said, were "callous, cold-blooded individuals" with "no sense of guilt or remorse." He went on to call for CEOs to be psychopath-screened, and the following year he and his checklist appeared in the terrific documentary *The Corporation.*

Public attention waned as the economy waxed in the middle years of the decade, but then returned with a vengeance after the global financial crisis of 2008. Hare and others reported in *Behavioral Sciences and the Law* that 4 percent of corporate managers met the psychopath threshold—compared to 1 percent of the general population. British businessman Brian Basham wrote in the *Independent* of an investment banker who once told him that his firm screened for psychopaths—in order to hire them! Apparently, "their characteristics exactly suited them to senior corporate finance roles." It makes you wonder about the poor regular folks at this bank, who presumably spent their days desperately trying to keep their empathy in the closet, acting like remorseless predators around their coworkers, all the while praying that a kind word wouldn't inadvertently slip out and reveal their secret humanity. (Come to think of it, this sounds like the way about 90 percent of straight men interact with one another.)

In the thoroughly enjoyable 2011 book *The Psychopath Test,* author Jon Ronson spends an afternoon going over the checklist with retired CEO Al Dunlap in his Florida mansion. Dunlap, nicknamed "Chainsaw" for the pure joy he seemed to take in firing tens of thousands of workers, was a darling of investors, and the day Chainsaw was named CEO of Sunbeam, company stock shot up 50 percent. Ronson and Dunlap sit in Chainsaw's Florida mansion—surrounded by ferocious sculptures of teeth-baring predators—as the author recites items from the psychopath checklist and the CEO reframes them as ideal qualities in the corporate world. It's a fun scene, especially if you were lucky enough to read it in the years before someone with this exact same personality became your president:

> "Grandiose sense of self-worth?" I said to Al . . . "No question," said Al. "If you don't believe in yourself, nobody else will. You've got to believe in you." . . . "Manipulative?" I said. "I think you could describe that as *leadership*," he said. . . . And so the morning continued, with Al redefining a great many psychopathic traits as Leadership Positives. Impulsivity was "just another way of saying Quick Analysis. "Some people spend a week weighing up the pros and cons. Me? I look at it for ten minutes. And if the pros outweigh the cons? Go!" Shallow Affect (an inability to feel a deep range of emotions) stops you from feeling "some nonsense emotions." A lack of remorse frees you up to move forward and achieve more great things. What's the point of drowning yourself in sorrow? "You have to judge yourself at the end of the day," he said. "Do I respect me? And if you do? Fine! You've had a great run."

Ronson dutifully points out that Chainsaw didn't score so highly on other parts of the test, but the similarities between traits that we revere in corporate leaders and fear in hitchhikers is striking. It isn't hard to picture some of our most notorious killers hitting the business lecture circuit: *How was I able to become the Son of Sam? I worked late nights, I didn't worry about winning popularity contests, and I never stopped listening to that voice inside my head!*

Ultimately, of course, the focus on individual villains lurking in the boardrooms misses the point. The problem resides in the business cycle, not the business psycho. There's a recession every decade, and each one uncovers a nest of crooks engaged in fraud that they thought would never be exposed because this would be the one time that the downturn wouldn't come, the money would keep coming in, and they would never get caught. The pattern of irrational behavior is too consistent to be attributed to individual deviants. The documentary *The Corporation* more helpfully proposes that it's business itself that is psychopathic. If corporations are people, as the Supreme Court's ludicrous *Citizens United* ruling claims they are, then they are "people" whose legal wiring drives them to seek maximum short-term self-interest at all times, regardless of the impact on others. They could take away your medicine or poison your food and not feel guilty in the slightest. On the contrary, their financial bloodstreams would be flooded with the endorphins and dopamine of rising share prices. Whether or not a given CEO is a so-called psychopath, she has to act like one in order to not be expelled from the corporate body like a foreign pathogen. I'm fine with labeling the people who sit atop our immoral and unequal economy with the slightly less clinical term "assholes," and I doubt anyone's holding their breath waiting for them to lead the anti-Trump resistance.

Many people think it's a different story when it comes to opposition inside the government. The opening months of the Trump administration saw a series of leaks from off-the-record bureaucrats and anonymous agents within our vast network of shadowy intelligence agencies insinuating Trump's involvement in numerous crimes and improprieties. But this form of resistance is very different from the potential popular power represented by the massive protests that at the same time were bringing together thousands—and sometimes even millions—of people in joyous defiance of the new president. I thoroughly enjoy the secret leaks and unattributed insider rumors about Trump that fill the news every day, but they also play right into his favorite narrative: that he's up against an array of powerful institutional forces determined to preserve the status quo.

Early in his presidency, as the *New York Times* and *Washington Post* ran weekly stories filled with embarrassing details, provided by dozens of leakers, about the new administration, Trump and his defenders started talking about a plot against the new president, coming from what they called the "deep state"—a term first used to describe the entrenched military rulers in countries like Turkey and Pakistan with a habit of overthrowing elected governments they don't feel like tolerating anymore.

"Deep state" is one of those terms people use to make themselves sound worldly and cynical, but it's actually kind of silly. There isn't a secret network of generals and death squads infiltrating all levels of US government, because there doesn't need to be. This is a country that has been able to create a perfectly "legal" gulag of thousands of prisons,* immigrant detention centers, and weaponized police precincts with full military divisions. One in thirty Americans lives under the shadow of the prison cell—either by being incarcerated or on parole or probation. Is it odd that Republicans claim to be for small government yet are led by someone who's all for increasing the power of armed government agents to trample over our consti-

---

* When the "Fact Checker" columnist for the *Washington Post* reviewed claims that the United States has around 5 percent of the world's population but 25 percent of its prison population, her first sentence was "This was a seemingly unbelievable figure that turned out to be correct."

tutional rights? Not really. Most Republicans who denounce "big government" love the repressive agencies that make up by far the biggest volume of government bureaucracy. What they think of as "government tyranny" are those additional nonviolent services taken on by twentieth-century governments around the world in response to popular demand: caring for the elderly and the sick, monitoring discrimination and the safety of the food supply, and so on.

While the conservative media rails against the invisible forces of the "deep state" conspiring against Trump, it's the members of the quite visible repressive state that might be his strongest base of support. He was endorsed by unions representing Border Patrol and immigration agents and officers in many police departments. Compared to the hundreds of articles written about white male factory workers in the Midwest, there's been little attention paid to the votes Trump got from millions of cops, military lifers, and deporters—including the frightening ways he might embolden some of the most racist and sexist among them. Trump's appeal to these agents of law enforcement is that they don't have to be bound by any laws themselves: No more federal oversight of police departments that keep killing unarmed Black people. No more military rules requiring soldiers to adhere to international laws against torture and abuse. No more directives to immigration agents about whom they can and can't lock up and deport.

During the controversy over FBI chief James Comey's decision to publicly criticize Hillary Clinton's use of a private email server in the months leading up to the election, a revealing article in the *Washington Post* by Republican operative Ed Rogers explained the internal pressures on Comey:

> There are steady rumors floating around that the FBI doesn't trust the Justice Department. The FBI views itself as a crime

fighter, and many rank-and-file agents think of their political bosses at DOJ as social tinkerers who are obsessed with the Black Lives Matter movement, transgender bathroom breaks and the like; that they really don't "get" law enforcement.

Given all this, there was no way Comey could have let the original investigation end with a benign written statement saying there were no grounds for an indictment or prosecution. One former agent told me that Comey was facing somewhat of an insurrection if he let the investigation be swept under the rug. So he had to publicly explain the bureau's work and defend the independence and credibility of America's premier law enforcement organization.

In other words, there are many supposed law enforcement agents in the FBI who don't view civil rights violations and extrajudicial police murders of people of color as "real" laws that deserve their attention. Like many cops, Border Patrol, and ICE agents, they don't even pretend to serve and protect democracy. They respect power and hunger for authority. This is the actual everyday state: not deep but brutally shallow. And the same is true in the government's upper levels, where the early conflicts with the Trump administration are primarily turf battles between bureaucratic infighters who have far more in common with each other than they have with any of us.

While Trump posed for pictures with cops, Hillary Clinton proudly campaigned on her deep wells of support in the ruling class in the mistaken belief that most Americans considered that an asset. She invited billionaires to speak onstage at her campaign rallies, from Democrats like Warren Buffett to Republicans like former New York City mayor Michael Bloomberg. Her campaign eagerly coordinated the endorsement of dozens of Bush administration war criminals—the very people most Democratic voters furiously protested just a decade earlier—and reportedly even courted Bush family donors with the claim that Clinton better "represents their values." If official politics keeps moving rightward, there's no telling whose endorsements Chelsea Clinton will seek for her inevitable future run: George Zimmerman? Scott Baio?

Trump had some billionaires in his camp, too, but not the kind who clean up well for public appearances. He attracted the likes of Sheldon Adelson, a slimy casino magnate who claims that Palestinians "are a made-up people," and eighty-seven-year-old oil magnate T. Boone Pickens, who gave the endorsement of the campaign when he declared, "I'm ready to take a chance on [Trump]. And just in case it's a mistake, [I'll] be gone."

Then there's Trump's most important backer, the hedge fund billionaire and socially awkward recluse Robert Mercer, who followed his buddy Steve Bannon into the Trump camp. According to the *New Yorker*'s Jane Mayer, Mercer is an avid peddler of conspiracies about Bill and Hillary Clinton being drug runners and murderers, and he's a devoted follower of Arthur Robinson, a crackpot scientist who argues that radiation from nuclear attacks and spills might be good for people.

Overall, however, the vast majority of billionaires, CEOs, military strategists, and power brokers in both parties didn't like Trump, not so much for his crude sexism and racism or his incompetence as for his lack of class loyalty. He's a billionaire (supposedly), but as a member of that club, he's a bit of a renegade. After a lifetime of receiving (earned) disrespect from the leading lights of business, culture, and politics, Trump shows little deference to them or any of their institutions, customs, or prior agreements. He's fine tearing up their treaties and trade agreements, and ignoring their protocol for interactions with the press and foreign leaders. While Bernie Sanders dutifully campaigned for Clinton even as the dirty tricks used by her campaign against him were coming to light, nobody would have been surprised if Trump had decided to launch an independent run in the event that he didn't win the Republican nomination. Most of us are used to not being able to trust our politicians, but for rich people this is a new and unsettling feeling.

Yet this oligarchy that has such power over most of our lives was unable to stop Trump from winning, and they even helped put him in office despite themselves. It's the latest step in the American ruling class's long devolution from the captains of industry who spent the twentieth century building a political and economic juggernaut and global postcolonial empire into our day's myopic band of mega-rich parasites and antisocial libertarians who scavenge the remains of our pensions and public wealth in what Matt Taibbi memorably calls a "griftopia":

> What has taken place over the last generation is a highly complicated merger of crime and policy, of stealing and government. Far from taking care of the rest of us, the financial leaders of America and their political servants have seemingly reached the cynical conclusion that our society is not worth saving and have taken on a new mission that involves not creating wealth for all, but simply absconding with whatever wealth remains in our hollowed-out economy. They don't feed us, we feed them.*

What the hell happened? The liberal explanation can be summed up in the response by Congresswoman Nancy Pelosi to a college student's question about why Pelosi and the Democratic Party supported capitalism:

....

* *Griftopia* came out in 2010, and its angle of "I'm a cynic and I still can't believe this shit they're pulling off" is indicative of how the 2008 financial crisis demolished the credibility of the US ruling class in the eyes of millions.

About forty years ago, no less a person than the chairman of Standard Oil of New Jersey talked about "stakeholder capitalism"—capitalism that said when we make decisions as managements and CEOs of the country, we take into consideration our shareholders . . . our workers, our customers and the community at large. At that time, the disparity between the CEO and the worker was about forty times more for the CEO than the worker. As productivity rose, the pay of the worker rose and the pay of the CEO . . . rose together.

Around twenty years ago, it started to turn into "shareholder capitalism" where we're strictly talking about the quarterly report. So a CEO would make much more money by keeping pay low, even though productivity is rising. The worker is not getting any more pay, and the CEO is getting big pay because he's kept costs low by depriving workers of their share of the productivity they've created. . . . The disparity between the CEO and the worker under "shareholder capitalism" is more like 350 to 400 to 1.

The problem with this explanation—capitalism worked for everybody when capitalists were nice, but then they stopped being nice—is that it doesn't explain anything. If you watched *Mad Men,* you'll know that the time when corporate ruthlessness started to rise—the early 1970s—was right when the execs were going to consciousness-raising sessions and exploring their inner hippies. By contrast, inequality was much lower in the 1950s, when Fortune 500 boardrooms were at their most square and conservative. It had nothing to do with whether CEOs thought of themselves as shareholders or stakeholders—and everything to do with the fact that more workers were in unions at the time, and more of those unions were willing and able to go on strike to increase their members' share of the overall pie. Today, companies like Uber call their employees *partners* and refer to themselves as part of a *sharing economy*—phrases that would have made a 1950s suit want to puke. But that executive would quickly get over his disgust and admire Uber's growth into a nonunion behemoth on the backs of drivers who often work fourteen-hour days and sleep in parking lots because they can't afford to live anywhere near city centers.

Just as the decline of the labor movement eased the economic pressure on our ruling class, the end of the Cold War allowed them a lot more political wiggle room. The intense ideological rivalry with the Soviet Union imposed some serious discipline to at least keep up the appearance that Western capitalism produced a superior society. When civil rights protests in Mississippi exposed the horrors of segregation, or when army propaganda about Vietnam turned out to be blatant lies, there was a price to be paid in the great game for international hearts and minds. Since the fall of the Berlin Wall, the ruling class has slowly discovered, to its great relief, that the price of American corruption, hypocrisy, and cruelty has gone way down. These days, Congress can shut down the government over a budget dispute, the presidential election can be stolen, and cops can murder people on camera without missing a single paycheck, and the response from the most powerful Americans is at most to sadly shake their heads as they click back onto the business news. Like addicts, they've been unable to rise out of their stupor of taking all our money to do anything about the steady decline of their government's legitimacy.

And now we've reached the new low of president Donald Trump, a man who doesn't even pretend to care about his country's noble tradition of putting on an elaborate show of following the rule of law. An older, dimmer, and slouchier composite of various dictators around the world, Trump rails against American decline while being its most damning embodiment. The ruling class found him just as revolting as the rest of us did, but to their horror they saw the very undemocratic structures that keep us peasants in our place—the Electoral College, voter suppression, a rigid two-party system with one party that has gone berserk, and so on—working to elevate this renegade directly into power.

Eh, they'll get used to it. They'd rather not feel embarrassed after every White House meeting with a foreign dignitary, and they'd feel more at ease with a president who didn't demand his staff reduce all policy papers to "a single page, with lots of graphics and maps," as the *New York Times* gleefully reported, but they'll dig the tax cuts. Some of them may wince at the sadism of the immigration raids at schools and hospitals, but they'll benefit from a labor market where millions of undocumented workers cling to their jobs in a state of fear. So they'll take a deep breath and play along. They'll let the president take credit for their decision to hire five hundred workers and do him the favor of not mentioning their decision to fire six hundred the week before. And they'll sincerely wish the president would stop denying climate change, but they'll find it hard to rouse themselves to action while all that increased oil and gas production drives down their energy costs and sends the stock market to new heights, even as the stock exchange itself begins to slowly submerge beneath the incoming waters of New York Harbor.

PART III

Socialism: Government by and for the People

8

We the Democracy

he shock of Trump's election win unleashed a legion of Internet threads about how our universe must have taken a
detour into some alternate reality (the Cubs winning the World
Series a week earlier didn't help). Here's my version: maybe we're
all subjects in a cosmic psychology study, like the Milgram experiment that tested if people would obey orders to administer
horrible electric shocks just because an authority figure in a white
coat told them to. What if this is all a hoax to find out what happens when the greatest authority figure in the world is a jackass
that most people wouldn't trust to pay back ten bucks? What will
Americans do when he says he's barring people from seven predominantly Muslim countries, based on classified information we
don't get to see? Would they be good loyal citizens and follow
along if he started a war just to boost his ego when he's feeling hurt
by negative cable news coverage?

If Trump's presidency actually were a test to measure blind obe-
dience, I'm sorry to say that in the initial days after his election, many
leaders of our so-called opposition party would have passed that test
with flying colors. From Clinton and Obama to even Bernie Sanders

and Elizabeth Warren,* the talking points in November 2016 were that Democrats would "seek common ground" with the new groper in chief and "root for the success" of someone they had just campaigned against as a fascist who needed to be stopped. Thankfully, most of their voters had precisely the opposite reaction, and their immediate resistance has been a defining feature of the beginning of the Trump Era. From the tens of thousands who took to the streets on the day after his election to the three million who came out to the Women's March in Washington, DC, and around the country on the day after his inauguration, people made it clear from the jump that they were not going to give Trump the respect he doesn't deserve.

And then came a critical showdown: the spontaneous protests in dozens of airports demanding that stranded travelers from seven predominantly Muslim countries be allowed to enter the country. Possibly the largest and most important protest against Islamophobia in American history, the "uprising at the airports" drastically shifted the political terrain and almost certainly played a role in giving judges the confidence to strike down Trump's travel ban. We can only hope that these early resistance actions will ultimately turn out to be as fateful for Trump's reign as the secret meeting with bank leaders was for Obama's, but it's already clear that things would look far worse if ordinary people had followed the pathetically placid lead of their elected officials.

Trump responded to this widespread opposition with the same denunciations of #FakeNews and #PaidProtesters he tossed

....

* Sanders: "If Mr. Trump has the guts to stand up to those corporations [that move jobs overseas] he will have an ally with me."
Warren: "When President-elect Trump wants to . . . increase the economic security of middle-class families, then count me in. I will put aside our differences and I will work with him to accomplish that goal."

around during the campaign. But once he was president, he had a new argument:

> Watched protests yesterday but was under the impression that we just had an election! Why didn't these people vote? Celebs hurt cause badly.

That was @realDonaldTrump's Sunday morning tweet after the Women's March, and beyond the random shot at celebrities (coming from the biggest starfucker in the world), his message was clear: he somehow won this democracy thing, so protesting him is therefore antidemocratic. This kind of reasoning is ominous coming from a president who makes no secret of his fondness for authoritarian leaders. As far back as 1990, he expressed creepy admiration for the Chinese government's notorious repression of the Tiananmen Square protests the year before:

> When the students poured into Tiananmen Square, the Chinese government almost blew it. Then they were vicious, they were horrible, but they put it down with strength. That shows you the power of strength. Our country is right now perceived as weak . . . as being spat on by the rest of the world.

But, as I've argued, Trump's limited view of democracy is in many ways simply a blunter expression of conventional wisdom that's usually more delicately put: *Go out and protest if you want, but you'll have to wait for the next election to make real change.* Trump's presidency poses a challenge to this logic. A majority of the country hasn't supported him from the first day, and a significant section of that majority doesn't want to wait four years while their immigrant neighbors are deported, doesn't think we can afford to wait four years as the planet gets hotter, and isn't completely sure if we wait four years that Trump won't have somehow declared himself president for life. That last one may sound a little far out, but remember, the Cubs won the World Series.

And so there are now millions of people who, until recently, understood their involvement in politics to be voting every two to four years (if that) who now see themselves as part of "the resistance" to a president under whose reign the normal rules can't apply. This is an important development that can represent so much more than a bunch of bodies to knock on doors in 2018 and 2020 to "take back" Congress and the White House for a bunch of politicians who want to "go back" to a status quo that none of us liked. Mass participation in politics can instead lead to building the unions and protest organizations that have potential not only to stop Trump but also to lay the basis for a democracy more worthy of the name.

Democracy is a Greek word that means rule by the people, or *demos*. In ancient Athens, where democracy was most fully developed, most important government positions were rotating posts filled by random selection among the population, most of whom were not rich philosophers like Plato (who absolutely hated this system, by the way). In fact, the word *demos* means both the people in general and, more specifically, the majority class of peasants. Non-Athenian slaves were excluded, which is a very large asterisk, but the important fact remains that in the original form of democracy, poor citizens led society on more equal footing with rich citizens than we in the modern world can fully imagine.

That's probably why ruling classes considered democracy to be a terrible idea for most of the next two thousand years, until the *demos* rose up in revolutions across Europe and the Americas in the eighteenth and nineteenth centuries, and, in the United States and France, elites were forced to reconcile themselves to some form of popular participation in government. As the word *democracy* started to come back into popular usage in the 1800s, it had a revealingly wider set of meanings than today's limited definition of a form of government with elections.* Democracy meant that, but it could also mean the popular will, egalitarianism, mass protest movements, or, simply, the people. The Chartists in England—the first large-scale working-class movement in history, which emerged in the 1830s and '40s—often referred to themselves simply as "the democracy." You can hear an echo of this idea in the popular protest chant "This is what democracy looks like!"

But, for the most part, that wider meaning of the word was lost, as the democracy that emerged in the modern world was not defined, as per the ancient Greeks, as the political rule by the majority class. Instead, modern democracy came to be primarily defined in terms of individual rights and liberties—a tradition that, as the brilliant socialist historian Ellen Meiksins Wood explains in *Democracy Against Capitalism*, evolved from the fight of medieval lords, codified in documents like the Magna Carta, to protect against kings' infringing on their hereditary privileges over their land and peasants. Over the past two hundred years, the struggles to win the right to vote and to free speech have transformed these once elite privileges into our modern conception of democratic rights, and this is one of the great advances in modern history. But we need to revive the Chartists' class definition of democracy, because the strength of our individual rights has always depended on our collective strength as workers, as women, as African Americans, and so on.

With Trump in the White House, all of us now find ourselves facing the situation that has been true in many statehouses for years: a government of hard right–wingers who don't represent the

* I learned this and so much more from volume 1 of Hal Draper's incredible series *Karl Marx's Theory of Revolution*.

majority of their population but derive their authority from voter suppression, gerrymandering, and vast popular disillusionment with politics. For young people in particular, this government isn't just unrepresentative, it seems to come from a different planet. Members of the so-called millennial generation overwhelmingly support immigrant rights, the Black Lives Matter movement, and transgender people's right to use the bathroom they prefer. But they're stuck in a country held hostage by an aging white Republican minority that genuinely believes Barack Obama is an undercover Muslim, immigration is a plot to make America less white, and two people with similar genitalia can't really love each other.

Throughout history, the combination of politically frustrated youth and an out-of-touch and unresponsive government has been a potentially explosive situation, and Trump and the Republicans know they need to clamp down on dissent. They'll spread fake news about immigrant voter fraud to strip more people of the right to vote, empower police to crack down harder on demonstrations, and pressure campus administrators to suspend and expel student activists. Critical aspects of whatever freedoms and liberties we have in this country will be up for grabs in the coming years.

But in order to defend democracy from Trump we'll have to create more of it. We'll need to assert our right to vote—and work to give ourselves choices beyond Donald versus Hillary, Trumpcare versus Obamacare, deporting millions of immigrants versus deporting even more millions of immigrants. We'll have to challenge the legitimacy of Trump's authority—and of police officers who break the law every day and lie about it afterward as brazenly as their hero president. And as we fight his attempts to consolidate power, we can't rely on Democrats to stand with us—even when it seems to be in their obvious self-interest, like fighting to stop an election from being stolen from them.

In the midst of the electoral chaos in 2000, Al Gore's campaign actively discouraged its supporters in the labor and civil rights movements from fighting back. Union organizer Jane McAlevey recalls, in her book *Raising Expectations (and Raising Hell)*, that activists were on the ground in Florida waiting for the call to mobilize, only to be told that leading Democratic Party officials "don't want to protest. They don't want to rock the boat. They don't want to seem like they don't have faith in the legal system." They kept proclaiming that faith even after the legal system gave them the infamous *Bush v. Gore* ruling that stopped the Florida recount. "The state was Gore's to lose," concludes McAlevey, "and the absolute determination with which the labor elite and the Democratic Party leadership crushed their own constituents' desire to express their political passions cost us the election."

Democrats preferred to sacrifice their own presidential victory rather than unleash potentially explosive protests that might have (rightfully) led millions to question the legitimacy of their elections. And they did the same on a smaller scale in 2016 when they downplayed reports of fraud and voter suppression in order to find that "common ground." When people whose entire careers are devoted to political campaigns think it's better to forfeit the biggest race of them all for the sake of preserving the façade of free and fair elections, our goal should be to tear down that façade and set our sights on a fuller democracy that can only be fulfilled in a society actually run by We the Demos.

9

Can't Go Left
if You're Stuck in the Middle

We strongly recommend focusing on defense against the Trump agenda rather than developing an entire alternative policy agenda. Defining a proactive agenda is time-intensive, divisive, and, quite frankly, a distraction, since there is zero chance that we as progressives will get to put our agenda into action at the federal level in the next four years.

This advice comes from the *Indivisible Guide*, the online protest manual from former Democratic Congressional aides that was downloaded by millions of people in the months after Trump's election. Facing Republican control of the White House and both houses of Congress, the *Indivisible Guide* laid out a resistance plan modeled on the tactics used by the Tea Party to pressure local Congress members to oppose everything Obama tried to do, and it was a smashing success. Indivisible Committees have sprung up in hundreds of cities to mobilize for town hall meetings that, as I write these words, are having a real effect in thwarting Republican plans to replace Obama's inadequate health insurance law with an almost unimaginably worse plan of their own.

But resistance alone will only get us so far. We have to find the time and space to simultaneously protest the policies that we stand against, and debate and decide what exactly it is that we're going to stand for. The *Indivisible Guide* authors might see these types of discussions as pointless daydreaming until the Democrats win back Congress and the White House, but many people don't share their faith in their former Capitol Hill bosses to come up with an "alternative policy agenda" on our behalf.

For the tens of millions who consider themselves socialists and are critical of the pro-business bias of the Democrats as well as the Republicans, now is absolutely the right time to start defining the agenda for a new left. About half the population—and a big majority of Democrats—supports expanding Medicare into a single-payer health care system. That means most of the Indivisible Committee members who confronted Republicans at town halls actually want something far more progressive than the Affordable Care Act. Imagine if some of these committees had issued press releases calling for a "Medicare for all" system while they were getting all that media coverage for defending the ACA: it could have started to put single-payer back in the national conversation. A PR consultant might warn that this is a confusing double message, but I disagree. Unlike the president of the United States, most people are capable of holding more than one thought at the same time.

This is also as good a time as any to establish the principles that should define us as a left. Bernie Sanders has become the country's most popular politician (which, admittedly, is about as meaningful as calling Ivanka the most normal Trump) because of his reputation for putting progressive values ahead of political opportunism. But that's exactly what he didn't do when he campaigned for Heath Mello, an antiabortion candidate in Nebraska. Sanders defended himself with the kind of Democratic double-talk that he's often so good at exposing:

> If we are going to protect a woman's right to choose, at the end of the day we're going to need Democratic control over the House and the Senate, and state governments all over this nation. And we have got to appreciate where people come from, and do our best to fight for the pro-choice agenda. But I think you just can't exclude people who disagree with us on one issue.

Got that? The only way to defend abortion rights is to have a Democratic majority, and the only way to have a Democratic majority is for the party to not stand united behind defending abortion rights. In a rather noticeable contrast to their behavior a year earlier, Democratic Party leaders rallied to Sanders's defense, and declared that the party had to be inclusive of antiabortion forces in order to avoid what the media derisively refers to as "ideological purity." As only liberals can, they framed their sellout as a noble defense of diversity and plurality: nobody will be excluded from our political party based on their political beliefs! Rather than use the Nebraska election to send a message that they wouldn't compromise in their defense of women's ability to control their own bodies, they declared that there's no compromise they won't make to win elections.

"You may not like the idea of being purely defensive; we certainly don't," write the authors of the *Indivisible Guide*. "As progressives, our natural inclination is to talk about the things we're for—a clean climate, economic justice, health care for all, racial equality, gender and sexual equality, and peace and human rights. These are the things that move us."

Somebody should have told that to Hillary Clinton, because the Wesleyan Media Project found that only 25 percent of her campaign ads focused on policy. That's far fewer than any other candidate in recent memory, including Donald Trump, who campaigned heavily on his racist and deceitful policies. Clinton's inclination was not at all "to talk about the things we're for" but to remind us for the thousandth time that her opponent was an unstable and hateful rogue, something that almost everyone—Trump supporters included—already knew.

And while from the day after Clinton lost, Democrats across the spectrum immediately felt free to admit that she was a terrible candidate who didn't make it clear what she stood for, the party as a whole is essentially continuing the strategy of her disastrous campaign: standing for as little as possible, hoping that Trump will be brought down by his own incompetence, and hoping that they will be rewarded as the more responsible group to oversee the grossly unequal and dysfunctional system that people revolted against in the first place.

It's easy to make fun of the blunt simplicity of "America First." But in politics it's a good thing to have uncomplicated ideas, not because people are dolts who can't understand complexity, as too many liberals smugly assume, but because it means you just might actually stand for something. "Build a wall" is a ridiculously simple worldview, but what is the Democrats' alternative? An endless stream of empty phrases like *competing in the global economy* and *responsibly securing our borders* that perhaps sound intelligent and nuanced to people who are reasonably content with the way things are. In contrast, as Matt Taibbi wrote for *Rolling Stone* during the campaign, "The significance of Trump's wall idea, apart from its bluntly racist appeal as a barrier to nonwhite people, is that it redefines the world in terms of a clear Us and Them, with the politicians directly responsible for Us."

"The center core of what we believe [is] that we're a nation with an economy," declared Steve Bannon at the Conservative Political Action Conference (CPAC), "not an economy just in some global marketplace with open borders, but we are a nation with a culture and a—and a reason for being."

Those of us familiar with the Bannon canon hear the sinister racial implications of innocent sounding words like *nation* and *culture*. But we can also recognize that this is a dangerously effective critique of the political vision put forward by mainstream Republicans and Democrats alike, in which there is no "reason for being" other than the wildly unequal and unjust economy.

After decades of exploding economic inequality, popular frustration with that vision is bursting through around the world, and in most places the anti-immigrant right has been quicker than the left to offer a radical rejection of the status quo offered by mainstream parties of both the center-right and center-left. "For anti-systemic movements of the left in Europe, the lesson of recent years is clear," argues the Marxist writer Perry Anderson, from his vantage point in Britain. "If they are not to go on being outpaced by movements of the right, they cannot afford to be less radical in attacking the system, and must be more coherent in their opposition to it."

"Workers of the world unite" used to be our side's answer to "Build a wall." It's a slogan that says you're right to feel angry about the global race to the bottom, so let's team up with the people in other countries they're trying to pit us against and fight this system together. There are two obvious principles that should be the foundation for the left's approach to immigration: 1) All people deserve a living wage and equal rights, regardless of where they were born; 2) Human beings should be able to cross national borders at least as freely as the products they make and the companies they make them for. These principles are straightforward and moral, but they're not practical. Establishing true equality and freedom across borders would massively disrupt a global economic and political order that relies heavily on the borders and citizenship laws to divide us and mark some of us with second-class status—and that would be a good thing. We're supposed to be the ones who challenge the logic of global capitalism, not Steve Bannon, dammit.

If it sounds unrealistic to propose winning mass support for a world without borders, let me repeat that, as I write these words, a socialist is the most popular politician in the United States. Bernie started his presidential run with no name recognition outside his tiny home state of Vermont and finished it having won twenty-three states and more than thirteen million votes, which doesn't include states that had caucuses instead of primaries. He did it without taking money from corporations or SuperPACs and without watering down his politics. He did so well against all the odds precisely because his proposals to redistribute wealth by increasing taxes on the rich to fund universal health care and college education are radical, at least by the standards of current American politics.

Of course, Sanders lost the primaries to Clinton, in a process that we now know was actually as rigged as his supporters thought it was. It's easy to focus on the outright chicanery; the DNC working hand in glove with the Clinton campaign, CNN commentators passing her notes about upcoming debate questions, and so on. But even more important was the fact that Democratic Party insiders lined up almost unanimously against Sanders. While the media reported that the Clinton–Sanders race reflected a "divided party," the actual party was almost completely united—against Bernie. Hillary Clinton won 55 percent of the voter-based delegates in the primaries but 92 percent of the "superdelegates," made up of officeholders, apparatchiks, and big donors—a stunning reflection of the chasm between the party apparatus and the base that supports it.

The Republican primaries showed that, in the post–*Citizens United* era, power can shift from traditional party insiders (who almost universally didn't support Trump) to random eccentric billionaires like Robert Mercer, who can throw limitless amounts of cash that shift elections toward outsiders like Trump. But the Democratic primaries offered some different lessons, for better and for worse. Sanders showed that a viable grassroots campaign can be entirely funded by small donations, but his defeat showed that at least some political parties can't so easily be taken over from the outside. Throughout the primaries, the Clinton campaign tried to dismiss Sanders's platform as a utopian wish list—as if things like universal health care haven't existed in most wealthy countries around the world for decades. But these accusations did contain an ironic kernel of truth: Bernie's program *was* unrealistic—not the policies themselves but the idea that the rest of the party would ever support them and betray its corporate sponsors.

Can the left pull an inverse Tea Party, take over the Democratic Party, and turn it socialist? That's the goal for Sanders and many of his supporters. After he dropped out of the race, he announced a plan to transform the party in two ways: use the convention to make the platform more progressive and create a new generation of left-wing elected officials at all levels of government—nearly seven thousand people reportedly signed up to run for office after Sanders gave his speech. But platforms are meaningless in a party that doesn't hold candidates accountable to them—you know, like when you campaign for a guy who goes against the party's official position on abortion rights.

Similarly, anyone running for office can claim to be a "Sanders Democrat" if they find it advantageous, but Sanders never offered any specific criteria for what that would actually mean. Do you have to support single-payer health care? (Obviously, your stance on reproductive rights isn't going to be a sticking point.) More importantly, there is no reason to think that these new progressive

Democrats will break from the pattern of previous generations that started out to the left of the party mainstream but moved steadily to the right the higher they climbed the party ladder. Look no further than the pair who were hailed as the party's new progressive wing the year before Sanders started his presidential run. Massachusetts senator Elizabeth Warren refused to even endorse Sanders for fear of damaging her own clout within the party, while New York City mayor Bill de Blasio's biggest accomplishment has been staying out of jail for his many political kickback schemes.

Many progressives believe it's impossible to build a third party because of the undemocratic structure of the US political system and the dominant hold that the Democrats have over unions, civil rights organizations, and liberal nonprofits. There is a lot of evidence to support this argument—particularly the fact that the left hasn't created a major third party in more than a hundred years. But it's also true that during this period the strategy of running progressive candidates has failed to shift the party. The two shining moments in the history of the Democratic Party—Franklin Roosevelt's New Deal in the 1930s and Lyndon Johnson's Great Society in the 1960s—came about not because a bunch of lefties ran as down-ballot candidates and slowly took over the party from within, but because massive protest movements—sit-down strikes in the '30s and urban rebellions in the '60s—forced formerly moderate Democrats to shift hard to the left. Ironically, these shifts convinced a generation of socialists to then join the party, only to find themselves helpless, from the inside, to stop it from moving back to the center over the succeeding decades.*

....

* If you haven't yet learned much about the movements of the 1930s and 1960s, you'll be amazed by the heritage you've been denied when you read Howard Zinn's *A People's History of the United States*. For a deeper look at

It's not just a coincidence that the Democratic Party has been run by rich white guys for its entire two-hundred-year existence. The Democrats have long been "history's second-most enthusiastic capitalist party," as former Republican strategist Kevin Phillips once put it. Bernie-crats believe that the experience of 2016 is proof that the party should move left, but the Democratic establishment looks at the Republican Party being taken over by the Trump rump and sees a golden opportunity to finally be promoted to Corporate America's A-Team—as long as they make sure to not let those reckless socialists take over.

The Democratic Party isn't a monolith that's hostile to people with left-wing politics. It's actually much worse: a diverse and seemingly open organization that can become a very comfortable home for progressives by allowing them to win small policy battles at the cost of surrendering the larger war for their political souls. In exchange for the access to resources and exposure that progressives would never get from a third-party or independent run, Democrats demand complete loyalty to their rotten top-ballot candidates come election time, which, over time, fatally compromises the progressive message they started out with.

Bernie felt like he had to be a good soldier and campaign for Clinton even after she and the DNC kneecapped him—not just because he didn't want Trump to win but because his strategy for moving the Democratic Party leftward requires his not being excommunicated. So he claimed with a straight face that his political revolution "continues as Hillary Clinton seeks the White House."

....

how the Democrats coopted the movements of the '30s and '60s, check out Mike Davis's "The Barren Marriage of American Labor and the Democratic Party" (*New Left Review*) and Paul Heideman's "It's Their Party" (*Jacobin*), respectively.

As if Hillary Clinton has ever supported any revolution other than the planetary orbit around the sun—she's okay with that one because it leaves us in the same place year after year.

More importantly, by silencing his own criticisms of Clinton, Sanders left Donald Trump as the only voice expressing widespread disgust with Goldman Sachs and outrage over factory closures. Up to that point, Bernie's campaign showed that a genuinely left-wing campaign could inspire many more millions of people than a bland centrist one, a valuable lesson that will hopefully prove a sign of things to come. But until we find a way to build a socialist movement strong enough to exist independently of the Democratic Party, we'll keep getting trapped in the same cycle that always ends with the left collapsing into the middle, and all of politics being pushed farther to the right.

Hang on a second. Is this really the time to split our forces? Already the alarm is being sounded that the greatest threat to the tide of anti-Trump resistance is letting ourselves be divided. When it comes to our protests, it's true that we need maximum unity. The only way that so many millions of people could have participated in the historic Women's March on the day after Trump's inauguration was because it was inviting to women (and others) with a range of political opinions who wanted to take a stand against the sexism of the incoming president. We should aim for similarly broad coalitions in our neighborhoods and cities in response to Trump's immigration raids and budget cuts to our local public schools and hospitals. In these cases, unity is possible—and therefore necessary—because, as the *Indivisible Guide* says, there is broad agreement about what we're against.

The divisiveness that many liberals are warning against, however, isn't about protests but political campaigns—specifically the Democrats' efforts in the 2018 congressional elections and beyond.

This call for unity is about muffling the discussions about what it is that we're going to be for. If you think that's a cynical take, ask yourself when party leaders and their big-money sponsors have ever sacrificed *their* beliefs to build unity with the tens of millions of voters who desperately wanted them to oppose the Iraq War, force banks to suspend home foreclosures, or end deportations.

When young leftists aren't sure why they need to stay loyal to the Democrats, their elders sit them down and tell them a fable called "Ralph Nader: The Time We Flew Too Close to the Sun." According to legend, one day, millions of voters who were tired of the Democrats' pro-business politics under Bill Clinton arrogantly decided to back Nader's Green Party, which artificially lowered the rightful total of Clinton's successor, Al Gore, and gave the 2000 election to George W. Bush. The result was 9/11, the Iraq War, and a hundred other disasters that to this day serve as a reminder that good progressives must avoid the hubris of believing that we deserve our own party.

Fortunately, using modern scientific methods such as reading and counting, it's now possible to debunk many aspects of this folktale. Here's what we know: the election came down to an incredibly narrow 543-vote Bush win in Florida. It's true that Nader got 97,000 votes in the state, but it's also true that 200,000 Florida Democrats voted for Bush and that tens of thousands of Democrats—disproportionately African Americans—were wrongfully purged from the state's voting rolls. Oh, and Gore actually won Florida, but the Supreme Court blocked the recount and stole the election. Nader's running a fairly strong third-party campaign was actually one of the few aspects of the whole fiasco that was a sign of a healthy democracy—but the Democrats' subsequent hysterical scapegoating of Nader and the Greens made sure to end that.

Like an unbearable job interviewee who says his main weakness is that he sometimes just works too darn hard, Democrats like to tell themselves that their problem is that their voters are such intelligent free thinkers that it's hard for them to come together as effectively as the maniacally united Republicans. But you don't hear Republicans still whining about how Ross Perot's 1992 independent run split the Republican vote and gave the presidency to Bill Clinton. Nor did you hear them hyperventilating in 2016 about Trump's chances being threatened by the Libertarian run of Gary Johnson. Republicans don't have a greater love for democracy (certainly not when it comes to Black and Brown people being able to vote) but apparently understand that they have been made stronger by precisely what the Democratic Party is most afraid of, and the left most desperately needs: an open battle of ideas.

10

Solidarity Can Trump Hate

After Hillary Clinton lost to Donald Trump, most commentators concluded that one factor in her defeat was that the Democrats were no longer widely seen as fighters for the working class. In fact, this was acknowledged early in the campaign by Clinton ally and former DNC chair Ed Rendell, who told the *Washington Post*, "Will [Donald Trump] have some appeal to working-class Dems in Levittown or Bristol? Sure. For every one he'll lose one and a half [to] two Republican women." But somehow, the conversation about why Democrats didn't fight for workers quickly became a debate about whether the party should fight around "economic" or "social" issues. This is a classic Democratic move: pitting constituencies against each other like commuters trying to squeeze onto a rush hour bus. *Sorry, workers. We'd love to bring fighting factory closures on board but we're all filled up with making bathrooms gender-neutral. But don't worry. Try the next bus, should be arriving in four years.*

"Race versus class" is great for clickbait but usually horrible for understanding how oppression actually works in a world in which most workers aren't straight white men.* In the Memphis sanitation workers' strike of 1968 (where Martin Luther King was killed as he was organizing support), the Black workforce famously carried picket signs that read, "I Am a Man." If the Internet were around then, there would have been weeks of hot takes furiously debating whether the strikers were asserting their dignity as workers or African Americans, because obviously it had to be either one or the other.

In 2016, there was another strike by a predominantly Black workforce. A week before the election, members of Transport Workers Union (TWU) Local 234 in Philadelphia, the key Democratic stronghold in the "battleground" state of Pennsylvania, walked off the job to fight massive health care cost increases and weak safety provisions that allowed bus and train workers to be forced to work with as little as nine hours between shifts. But while Clinton is widely supposed to have over-emphasized so-called identity politics, she ignored the striking African American workers even as she found time for a celebrity rally at nearby Independence Hall with those noted Black icons Bruce Springsteen and Jon Bon Jovi. Yeah, she lost Pennsylvania.

US history doesn't alternate between periods of winning either racial or economic justice but periods of advancement in both or neither. When African Americans won their biggest victories—ending slavery in the mid-nineteenth century and ending segregation a hundred years later—it didn't take away rights from other people. On the contrary, those victories led to further struggles to increase rights for other groups, like women, immigrants, and workers. That's why Alicia Garza, one of the

---

* Keeanga-Yamahtta Taylor's *From #BlackLivesMatter to Black Liberation* is a great antidote to the toxic dichotomy of "race versus class."

creators of the #BlackLivesMatter campaign, has written, "When Black people get free, everyone gets free."

Conversely, times of great economic inequality like today are also times of great racial inequality. Those who argue that Democrats have ignored working-class concerns to focus on fighting for oppressed minorities seem to live in an alternate country, one that doesn't spy on Muslims, deny women both maternity leave and access to abortion, and imprison large numbers of Blacks and Latinxs. What the Democrats have done is help create a culture that doesn't tolerate certain bigoted words but passively shrugs at far more devastating structures of persecution. In *The New Jim Crow*, Michelle Alexander laid out the legal formula for racism that has replaced official segregation:

> The first step is to grant law enforcement officials extraordinary discretion regarding whom to stop, search, arrest, and charge for drug offenses, thus ensuring that conscious and unconscious racial beliefs and stereotypes will be given free rein. Unbridled discretion inevitably creates huge racial disparities.
>
> Then the damning step: Close the courthouse doors to all claims by defendants and private litigants that the criminal justice system operates in racially discriminatory fashion. Demand that anyone who wants to challenge racial bias in the system offer, in advance, clear proof that the racial disparities are the product of intentional racial discrimination—i.e. the work of a bigot. This evidence will almost never be available in the era of colorblindness, because everyone knows—but does not say— that the enemy in the War on Drugs can be identified by race.

Imagine if the rest of us had the same leeway in our jobs. A surgeon who left a scalpel inside a patient could face malpractice only if it could be proven that he did it out of malice. Kitchen workers could feel free to piss in the soup as long as they didn't actually say they hate yuppies. The subtitle of *The New Jim Crow* is *Mass Incarceration in the Age of Colorblindness*. More like "color-mute." African Americans are seeing their rates of discrimination and school segregation return to pre-1960s levels, but it's no longer legal for them to be told on the record that it's due to their race. And in return, it's no longer acceptable for Black folks to "play the race card." Cops can do whatever they want as long as they don't say (publicly) the N-word. (I can just imagine the catchy training slogan for new hires: *Don't say it. Pepper spray it!*) The American criminal justice system combines all the brutality of totalitarianism with the limp liberalism of a corporate diversity seminar.

Into this gross hypocrisy waded Donald Trump, demanding that we go back to the good old days, when it wasn't politically incorrect to talk about which women you wanted to sexually assault and you didn't have to pretend not to demonize whatever race or religion of people your country was at war with. Not since the Joker campaigned for mayor of Gotham City with the slogan, "Vote for me or I'll kill you" has there been such an openly hateful American politician. And the trolls have roared their approval and gained more confidence to harass and assault people in broad daylight.

In the days after Trump's election, the most popular slogan on the signs at vigils and rallies was "Love Trumps Hate." It made sense in that immediate moment, but we can't let that be the theme of our opposition—not because we should be ashamed of expressing love, but because its vagueness makes it a perfect rallying cry for shameless opportunists. It was Hillary Clinton, you may remember, who tried to present herself as the moral antidote to Trump's venom. "I believe what we need in America today is more love and kindness" was one of her campaign slogans, and she told *Buzzfeed*'s Ruby Cramer that her entire political career had been an attempt to "start a national conversation about basic human decency." Here are two heartwarming highlights from Hillary's end of that twenty-year conversation:

> They are not just gangs of kids anymore. They are often the kinds of kids that are called "super-predators." No conscience, no empathy. We can talk about why they ended up that way, but first we have to bring them to heel.
> —Supporting her husband's 1994 crime bill that put millions of ~~predators~~ human beings in prison

> They should be sent back as soon as it can be determined who responsible adults in their families are. We have to send a clear message that just because your child gets across the border doesn't mean your child gets to stay. We don't want to send a message contrary to our laws or encourage more to come.
> —Demanding in 2014 that refugee children fleeing horrible violence in Central America be deported, in violation of international law

If we are going to mount a strong resistance to Trump's plans to divide and conquer, we have to reject his bleak nationalist vision of a world of all against all, but that's not going to work with abstract and disingenuous calls for everyone to love one another. Instead we need to rebuild a culture of solidarity, the idea that people can unite across their differences not just because they are "nice" but because they have a common interest in not allowing themselves to be divided and conquered. As the old Industrial Workers of the World slogan puts it, "An injury to one is an injury to all."

Most of us are taught that the only way to get ahead in this society is to outcompete our neighbors, but while that might be true for businesses, it's never been true for ordinary people. The biggest gains for workers have come not through stabbing one another in the back to get ahead, but through uniting into unions to raise everyone's standard of living. Strikes have been rare in recent years, but when they happen, the corporate media act like puzzled anthropologists struggling to understand this strange behavior of workers willing to sacrifice many weeks' pay just to preserve the living standards of future hires—people they've never even met. Are they being tricked by their union leaders? Or outside agitators? No, they simply understand that by fighting for others they're also fighting for themselves—by refusing to allow the creation of a lower tier of workers who could someday be used to undercut them.

Solidarity is an idea, but it's also a tangible set of relationships and networks built on trust and reliability. A strike can't happen if one worker doesn't know if her coworkers will also walk off the job with her. Undocumented youth can only come out of the shadows unafraid if they are connected to organizations they can count on to defend them. When Trump tried to push through his first "Muslim ban," most of the thousands of people who flocked to JFK airport in Queens were not Muslim—but their protest helped give confidence to the city's Yemeni deli owners, who called a one-day strike to protest the ban the following week.

It's understandable to be skeptical about solidarity—especially when our efforts can seem like no match for the hatred that's now being expressed at the highest levels of government. That skepticism is often expressed in online articles or social media posts that dismiss efforts to show support for oppressed groups as little more than individuals trying to make themselves feel good. When we're by ourselves staring at a screen, these cynical dismissals can seem super radical, but often they're just missing the point. Yes, building solidarity feels good, precisely because it takes us out of our isolation and reminds us that we have common cause.

Creating solidarity is long-term work. The main obstacle isn't that people are so wedded to their ancient prejudices (although there's that). It's that we live in a world of false scarcity and enforced competition, where the resources exist for everyone to work twenty enjoyable hours a week and receive whatever level of higher education they desire, but we are made to fight like dogs for ourselves and our kids to be in the minority that has a chance at the good life. The oppressions that keep us divided aren't just bad ideas in our heads but structures that have to be overcome. As one example, cities aren't segregated simply because white people don't want to interact with Black people (although there's that) but because they've been afraid (correctly) that banks and realtors will literally lower the value of their house if the neighborhood is "too Black." As a result, building solidarity against racism doesn't just mean not being personally racist (although there's that) but requires joining collective efforts against the institutions that create and perpetuate racism.

These efforts take time, and trust has to be earned. Some Sanders supporters were disappointed that most African American primary voters—particularly those older than thirty—voted for Hillary Clinton despite the clear superiority of Sanders's track record and platform on racial justice. The most common media explanations for the Black vote in the primaries ranged from the illogical (African Americans didn't like Bernie's talk about economic justice) to the painfully condescending (Black folks just love the Clintons!) while ignoring the obvious (the Democratic Party machine is particularly strong in the Black community). A few national journalists who actually talked to Black voters got a more nuanced story: many Black voters liked Sanders's message but were uncomfortable putting their trust in someone they had just found out about, and they weren't sure they could trust him to mount a strong fight against the ever more frightening Republicans.

Nonetheless, Sanders made important inroads toward building a multiracial fight for wealth redistribution. But durable unity across racial lines will require more than just a progressive economic platform. At a time when violent racist attacks are on the rise—from police and civilians alike—unity will only be built by challenging the racism that divides us as well as working for policies in our common interest. One of the dangers of making elections the main focus of our work is that it pushes us toward trying to build the broadest possible party, which sounds reasonable but creates pressures to avoid "controversial" topics that might alienate some potential voters. That's how you end up with the sad sight of supposedly "socialist" parties in Europe pandering to rising xenophobia instead of fighting it.

Does this mean that the left shouldn't try to win over Trump supporters? It depends what you mean. Yes, we should try to convince some of the people who voted for Trump out of frustration that there's a better way to take on the elites. No, we shouldn't drop or downplay our focus on racism in order to connect with them on "economics," because the issues are completely intertwined. The struggles of white workers in deindustrializing areas of the Rust Belt are similar to the horrors that hit many Black and Latinx communities in the 1970s and '80s, but that wave of factory closures and drug epidemics was treated by Republicans and Democrats alike as a crisis of Black and Brown criminals and drug addicts, welfare queens, and deadbeat dads. Solidarity was missing then, and now the entire class is weaker for it.

The rise of openly racist far-right parties and politicians here and around the world marks a terrifying revival of some of history's most grotesque hatreds and a level of immorality that many people assumed humanity had evolved beyond. But we can't stand up to this bigotry by simply proclaiming love or human decency and pretending that the pre-Trump United States was a society based on love. If you can remember all the way back to a year ago, this was a country of skyrocketing inequality, alienation and hopelessness, live-streamed police murders and unseen drug overdoses, a country that reflexively bombed impoverished Muslim countries but shrank from the historic task of ending deadly climate change.

Donald Trump's message may seem like pure hate to those he is targeting and many more besides, but to the ordinary people whose votes he got last November, he's responded to a sham-loving society with a sham vision of solidarity—solidarity with only some people, not all. Socialists have real alternatives to offer—not the empty talk of togetherness coming from politicians funded by Wall Street bankers and military contractors that profit from our foreclosures and our deaths, but the strength of working people to unite in a common interest that is the opposite of Trump's message of hate and greed. And as people come together to defend one another from deportation and to assert our rights, more of us can discover and create the bonds of love and respect that can be the basis of a much stronger democracy than the crock that gave us Trump in the first place.

11

Beyond the Ballot Box

The Bernie Sanders campaign was a lightning bolt for the US left, which hadn't been having the best couple of decades. Only a few years earlier, politicians had been afraid to call themselves "liberal," yet suddenly people in seemingly unlikely places like Iowa and Idaho were lining up to show their fervent support for a socialist, with many of them telling pollsters that they considered themselves socialists, too. But wait—did many people become socialists because of Bernie, or did Bernie do so well because many people were already socialists? Undoubtedly, the answer lies somewhere in between. Either way, his campaign did us all a great service, but it's important to appreciate the degree to which the Sanders campaign didn't create the new potential for the American left so much as he revealed it.

Since at least 2011, polls have shown that a significant minority of the country prefers socialism to capitalism, with higher numbers among people who are young, Black, Latinx, or low-income. But because this desire for fundamental change had no representation in official politics, it lay buried for most of the Obama years, occasionally bursting into view with explosive protest movements.

Occupy Wall Street and the Movement for Black Lives dramatically changed the popular consciousness of economic and racial inequality, respectively, but both struggled to forge organizations with the durability and strength to win concrete gains. In different ways, both embraced models described as leaderless and decentralized; more accurately, both movements had informal leadership and power centers that made it hard to build the kind of large, active membership organizations necessary to endure the ups and downs of any protest movement. The advantage of these models was supposed to be that they would prevent co-optation, but, if anything, their lack of internal democratic structure made it easier for people running for office to claim the movements' support in exchange for little more than words. (It's especially ridiculous when politicians expect praise for simply saying "Black Lives Matter." The slogan's very point is to ironically pose the most minimal "demand" imaginable in order to expose the depths of American racism.)

Then came the Sanders campaign, which built on the foundation of these movements and others, such as the fifteen-dollar minimum wage campaign in cities like Seattle, and showed an entirely different way of popularizing left-wing ideas. His campaign not only reached a new audience, it also brought together people fighting around different issues with the very socialist theme that we're all on the same side, and provided an organization in which thousands could directly participate as volunteers and millions more could passively participate through their votes and donations.

Not surprisingly, many radicals are now looking to left-wing electoral campaigns, especially municipal races, as the key next step for building socialism. But if you agree with the points this book has been making about the severe limitations of our political process, you can see the flaws in this strategy. In a system that values democracy only to the extent that gets the people to affirm the direction in which our leaders are already planning to take us, socialists have to do a lot more than win elections. We have to build the power to back up our votes with action.

Back when Bernie Sanders was the mayor of Burlington, Vermont, he had a picture of Eugene Debs prominently displayed in his office. Your high school history class may have spent a minute on Debs, the guy who ran unsuccessfully for president five different times on the Socialist Party ticket in the early 1900s. Yet Sanders once said that this five-time loser was "probably the most effective and popular leader that the American working class has ever had," and he was absolutely right. Debs was a brilliant union organizer and the person who popularized socialism for the first time in this country among millions of his fellow workers.

Debs understood very well the role that elections could play in bringing about social change—and the role that they couldn't. "Voting for socialism," he famously wrote, "is not socialism any more than a menu is a meal." Debs used his presidential campaigns to barnstorm the country to give as many workers as possible a message precisely the opposite of what they heard from other candidates: that it would be not their vote but their collective power to shut down industry that had the power to transform society. "We should seek only to register the actual vote of socialism, no more no less," he wrote to his fellow socialists. "In our propaganda we should state our principles clearly, speak the truth fearlessly, seeking neither to flatter nor to offend, but only to convince those who should be with us and win them to our cause through an intelligent understanding of its mission."

Debs mainly wanted the votes of those who were already committed to the cause, not because he wanted ideological purity but because the movement he was trying to build could be achieved only through active and conscious organization. Workers must have unions powerful enough to take on their bosses economically in order to successfully challenge their parties politically, he wrote in the same article as quoted above, and those unions have to bring together workers of all races and nationalities "in the true spirit of solidarity, thus laying the foundation and developing the super-structure of the new system within the old." Without this strong foundation of social cohesion and economic power, he concluded, "the fruit of any political victories the workers may achieve will turn to ashes on their lips."

Bernie Sanders is part of the social democratic wing of the so-cialist tradition, which has always taken a rosier view than Debs about the potential of elections to bring about socialism. The glory days of social democracy were in much of Western Europe after World War II, a unique economic moment in history when an enormous post-war boom concentrated wealth in a handful of countries that were the centers of global capitalism, and the fear of communism pushed the elites in those countries into sharing some of that wealth with their working classes and their powerful labor movements. Social democrats in developing countries like Guatemala and Chile were brutally overthrown by CIA-backed coups, but in regions like Scan-dinavia they created impressive social welfare states that produced the most egalitarian societies with the highest living standards in the world. The hope was that these social democracies would pro-vide a model for the rest of the world to follow. Instead, as industry expanded to every continent, new economic powers emerged from China to Brazil, intensifying global competition, decreasing profit margins, and laying the basis for the dog-eat-dog capitalism some-times known as neoliberalism. Over the past few decades, social de-mocracies haven't been leading the way forward but getting dragged back down into the muck. Poverty and inequality are on the rise in Scandinavia, as are right-wing, anti-immigrant parties.

In my last book, *Socialism . . . Seriously*, I used the example of a famous 1989 Rolling Stones concert in Prague after the fall of the Berlin Wall to joke about the stifling cultural atmosphere of the supposedly "communist" countries in the old Eastern Bloc. What better indictment of Stalinist rule could there be, I asked, than one of the hippest cities in the world going crazy over the chance to see a bunch of aging rockers at least a decade past their prime? Like the Stones playing Prague, Bernie Sanders's campaign was a liberating experience for Americans, but also an indictment of just what a stifling political atmosphere we've endured for decades in the global center of anticommunism. We were so excited to finally get a chance to see social democracy perform, we didn't care if it was decades past its prime and increasingly seen across the ocean as hopelessly outdated.

The closest thing that the United States has seen to social democracy was the reforms begun by the 1930s New Deal policies of Franklin Roosevelt: Social Security, welfare, unemployment insurance, and a massive public works program to provide jobs during the Great Depression. Sanders has cited these programs as a model for his version of socialism, so it's useful to know that the key to winning them wasn't Roosevelt, a moderate Democrat from an aristocratic New York family, but the massive strikes and protests that convinced his government there was no other choice. As Roosevelt was running for president in 1932, thousands of unemployed veterans from the First World War camped threateningly in the parks of the capital city, demanding early payment of their war bonus. This "Bonus Army" dispersed only when General Douglas MacArthur led a regiment against them with bayonets and gas. Communists in cities like Chicago and New York organized unemployed councils to demand assistance and to break landlords' locks to move evicted families back into their homes—this happened tens of thousands of times in New York City in 1932 alone. Two years later, there were general strikes in Toledo, Minneapolis, and San Francisco. This was the type of "grassroots lobbying" it took to win the most important reforms of the twentieth century.

We don't have to go that far back for lessons that protests can win. Our side has lost more battles than we've won in recent decades, but we won gay marriage and ended the use of the death penalty in most states, and we did it not by finding candidates with those positions to run for office but by building movements that changed popular opinion and forced elected officials to change their positions. Single-payer health care has long been seen as the New Deal's missing piece. The way to win it won't start with finding a modern-day Roosevelt to lead us, but by figuring out the modern-day version of unemployed councils—imagine local committees occupying emergency rooms and dental offices to demand urgent care for the uninsured and underinsured.

Americans don't have a lot of experience with socialists running for office, but we can look abroad for more lessons. The most dramatic left-wing election victory in recent years happened in 2015 in Greece, where a small socialist coalition party called SYRIZA quickly grew in popularity and won office based on its call to reject the crippling debt repayments the country was being forced to make to European banks—while Greece's social democratic party was part of the discredited political establishment that had imposed horrible budget cuts to fund the debt repayment. The debt crisis, by the way, wasn't caused by Greeks borrowing money from their buddies across Europe, buying a bunch of flat-screen TVs, and then refusing to pay back their hardworking friends abroad. It happened because bankers in richer countries like Germany and France made lots of loans and investments—some solid, some shady—in smaller countries, including Greece, until enough of the shady ones helped trigger the 2008 global financial crisis. Then Greece was supposed to pay up.

SYRIZA's victory inspired hopes across Europe that finally someone would stand up to these crooked banksters. The new prime minister, Alexis Tsipras, believed that the "political revolution" of his party's stunning victory would impress European capitalists, but instead it enraged them. Like a clever fox negotiating with a concrete wall, Tsipras made concession after concession on SYRIZA's campaign promises, waiting in vain for Germany and the European and international financial institutions to respect the clear democratic will of the Greek people and meet them halfway, which, of course, they never did.

Desperate to change the terms of the game, Tsipras announced a national referendum on July 5 asking the Greek people to vote for or against the latest EU proposals for austerity, and 61 percent voted "Oxi!" (No!) The referendum was a startling moment for people in Greece and around the world, a glimpse of what something approaching actual democracy looks like, instead of the typical capitalist version of voting once in a while for which face you want to be getting the bad news from for the next few years. But while Oxi! was a powerful statement from the Greek people, words alone don't have the power to take on multinational banks.

Almost immediately after the referendum, Tsipras announced that he was going back to negotiations and was willing to accept most of the harsh measures that Greeks had just decisively voted down in the referendum he had called. In effect, Tsipras tried to use the mass democracy of Oxi! as a bargaining chip, but the EU responded to the referendum as it did to SYRIZA's election in January, by calling for even harsher austerity measures—including forcing the Greek parliament to pass a series of laws undoing every

SYRIZA promise and demanding that €50 billion in Greek assets be turned over to a fund controlled by the EU.

To the European bankers, all this voting was just a foolish attempt by the Greek people to resist the natural laws of capitalism. As is so often the case, the people in charge insisted that the crisis was a purely economic issue of debt repayment, rather than a political question of who gets to decide which debts are paid and who has to pay them. In the country that introduced democracy to the world 2,500 years ago, banks and their political lackeys attempted to declare the concept null and void. The Greek elections exposed the bankers' laws as not natural at all. But to overturn those laws and replace them would have required SYRIZA to use its votes to organize widespread strikes and resistance to take the fight to a higher level.

The Greek experience is a stark illustration of a point that Friedrich Engels made about elections more than a hundred years ago, when Europeans were still fighting for the right to vote:

> Universal suffrage is the gauge of the maturity of the working class. It cannot and never will be anything more in the modern state, but that is enough. On the day when the thermometer of universal suffrage shows boiling point among the workers, they as well as the capitalists will know where they stand.

Engels's point was that while socialists should use whatever limited democracy is available to put out their message, capitalism isn't going to allow itself to simply be elected out of existence. As Eugene Debs said, you can't just order a better world like it's takeout. If we want to live in a more authentic democracy, we'll have to make it ourselves.

12

Our Revolution

We grow up being taught that democracy and capitalism are partners, when in fact they're bitter rivals. One calls for a society in which each person owns an equal share, while the other depends on a small minority owning more than the rest of us combined. One believes that decisions affecting our world should be publicly debated and put up to a vote. The other assesses all decisions according to whether or not they will make money for the small minority, who give themselves the pompous title The Free Market, like a horrible jam band that plays at Stanford frat parties.

There's a great takedown of market mythology in Robert Reich's *Saving Capitalism*. Reich, an economics professor and former labor secretary under Bill Clinton, was one of the few prominent figures from the liberal wing of the Democratic Party to endorse Sanders. It might seem odd that someone who wants to save capitalism would support a candidate who famously calls himself a socialist. But the capitalism that Reich wants to rescue isn't our present system of spiraling inequality. He wants a more just and democratic version of it, summarized in the book's subtitle: *For the Many, Not the Few*. This "saved" capitalism is similar to what Sanders calls "democratic socialism": a defense and, ideally, expansion of the social welfare programs of the twentieth century, namely Social Security, Medicare, and their more robust European counterparts.

Reich's most important insight is that capitalism is not a god impartially ruling over humanity but a creation of human society that can and should be altered as we see fit. "The 'free market' does not exist in the wilds beyond the reach of civilization," he writes. "Competition in the wild is a contest for survival in which the largest and strongest typically win. Civilization, by contrast, is defined by rules; rules create markets, and governments generate the rules. . . . Government doesn't 'intrude' on the 'free market.' It creates the market." It's people, not natural law, who have decided that corporations can use bankruptcy law as a means to cut workers' pensions, while homeowners can't use it to reduce their mortgage payments. But not all people—only a select few have a real say over those kinds of questions. The workers and farmers of Mexico, the United States, and Canada certainly didn't have a say in creating the rules of the North American Free Trade Agreement (NAFTA), which enriched the wealthy of all three countries at the expense of their general populations.

Even a concept as seemingly natural as private property is actually the result of a series of laws and rules. Ownership, Reich explains, might seem as obvious as "I bought this" or "I created that," but there are all sorts of things that most societies have decided you're not allowed to own: from dirty bombs to cooking recipes to other human beings. We could make a similar decision about life-saving drugs, but instead, the United States gives pharmaceutical companies longer patents than any other country, and our "free market" doesn't allow us to buy cheaper drugs abroad. The point is, Reich argues, that "we need not be victims of impersonal 'market forces' over which we have no control."

Saving Capitalism offers a set of proposals for us to take control over the market and make capitalism more equal, from raising the minimum wage and making it easier for workers to form unions to forcing corporations to pay higher taxes if their ratio of CEO-to-worker pay is higher than that of others. The final idea is a guaranteed income that all adults could comfortably live on, so that the mechanization of many jobs doesn't lead to mass poverty. Reich takes on the standard right-wing objection that this would lead to widespread laziness, insisting instead that it would enable many more people to pursue socially valuable work in fields like education and the arts.

It's refreshing to see an economist putting forward radical ideas, but we should be clear about something that Reich apparently isn't. A guaranteed livable income wouldn't save capitalism but threaten its existence, because if we already have enough money to meet our basic necessities, why would any of us subject ourselves to going to work for a boss? Capitalism is driven by the quest for profits—the extra money left over after a company has paid its employees and various other expenses. Profit is the result of exploitation—of workers producing more wealth than they are paid for their labor. Workers only enter this arrangement because they have no other choice to pay the bills: they have to work for a boss because they don't have the resources to own a company—and they don't live in a society with a guaranteed income. Don't get me wrong. The fact that a universal income is a threat to capitalism only makes me support it more. But this hole in Reich's logic is symptomatic of a larger blind spot to the class antagonism that exists at the heart of capitalism and makes it inherently undemocratic and unequal.

Capitalism has two spheres: production and distribution. Reich offers many insights into how the "free market" creates unequal rules for the distribution of wealth, but not into the equally skewed rules that dictate how that wealth is created in the first place. In a chapter about contracts, for example, he explains the bogus "consent" given by Apple users when they click "I Accept" and sign away privacy rights in order to use the iCloud. "As a practical matter," Reich writes, "you didn't have a choice because every other service has the same terms." But there is no similar chapter about how the workers who make Apple products—like other blue- and white-collar workers for companies the world over—have little choice about accepting unfair pay and working conditions, and no choice at all about what is done with the products they create. Reich could just as easily note that as a practical matter, these workers don't have a choice because every other employer offers the same terms—or worse, if they're unemployed.

This lack of choice for the vast majority of humanity is necessary for the functioning of capitalism—which is why it can never be reformed into a system that works "for the many." But here again Reich's main point can be extended. If it's possible for human beings to change the rules they've created governing the terms of ownership for cooking recipes and drug patents, it's also possible for us to decide that the companies that produce and distribute wealth shouldn't be privately owned but collectively run by their workers and consumers. The heart of socialism isn't that wealth should be equally distributed to the people but that the people should democratically decide and control how that wealth is created.

Workers' control is vital to socialism not just because it's a nice idea, but because workers are the only force with the potential power to bring it about. Reich puts forward a vision of US history in which equality and justice have been advanced by progressive presidents, as opposed to by the strikes and sit-ins that forced them into action. *Saving Capitalism* argues that unions and grassroots organizations need to be supported because they are a "counterveiling power" that can balance out the self-serving interests of corporations and the 1 percent. But the Flint Sit-Down Strikers and Montgomery Bus Boycotters didn't risk everything and sacrifice dearly so that one day their children could fight the same damn battles as part of an eternal counterweight to greedy owners and racist segregation. They fought to win a more just society forever—and many of them were clear that this society needed to be socialist.

At different points over the last century, strikes and protests have exploded into mass movements involving tens of millions, creating genuinely revolutionary moments in which the democratic control of society became a real possibility. The Russian revolutionary Leon Trotsky memorably explained how these moments are the potential beginning for a society that is actually ruled by the *demos*:

> The most indubitable feature of a revolution is the direct interference of the masses in historical events. In ordinary times the state, be it monarchical or democratic, elevates itself above the nation, and history is made by specialists in that line of business—kings, ministers, bureaucrats, parliamentarians, journalists.
>
> But at those crucial moments when the old order becomes no longer endurable to the masses, they break over the barriers excluding them from the political arena, sweep aside their traditional representatives, and create by their own interference the initial groundwork for a new régime.
>
> Whether this is good or bad we leave to the judgment of moralists. We ourselves will take the facts as they are given by the objective course of development. The history of a revolution is for us first of all a history of the forcible entrance of the masses into the realm of rulership over their own destiny.

Trotsky was writing about the most famous revolution of the twentieth century, which in Russia in 1917 created a new form of government based on workers' councils or *soviets*. Because this type of class-based democracy is fundamentally at odds with capitalism, the revolution was either going to spread or (spoiler alert) be overturned—isolated by foreign invasion and destroyed by a new hierarchy led by Joseph Stalin. Today the Russian Revolution is often described as a coup. Never mind that it was led and passionately fought for by millions of workers, soldiers, peasants, and students—it was undemocratic because it didn't happen through elections. By this logic the American Revolution was wrong because George Washington and company didn't try to campaign for independence inside the British parliament, and the Civil War was an immoral conspiracy of enslaved Black people violating the laws of bondage that had been democratically approved. Revolutions happen when political systems cannot legally accommodate desperately needed change, and they've been one of the most important methods for moving history decisively forward, from ending the rule of monarchies in Europe to winning independence from colonialism in the Americas in the nineteenth century and across Africa and Asia in the mid-twentieth century.

In 2011, revolutions spread across the Middle East and North Africa in a wave that became known as the Arab Spring. Egypt saw the largest of these revolutions, in which millions of people took to the streets for weeks to fight off police and hired thugs to overthrow the thirty-year reign of the US-backed dictator Hosni Mubarak. During the Arab Spring, longstanding divisions and repressive traditions were suddenly examined in a new light as ordinary people were thrust into a situation in which their ideas mattered. Every day there were scenes that brought to mind the Russian socialist Vladimir Lenin's famous quote about revolutions:

"There are decades where nothing happens; and there are weeks where decades happen." Here is how the *New York Times* described a center of the revolution in Yemen:

> In the sprawling tent city outside Sana University, rival tribesmen have forsworn their vendettas to sit, eat and dance together. College students talk to Zaydi rebels from the north, and discover they are not, in fact, the devils portrayed in government newspapers. Women who have spent their lives indoors give impassioned speeches to amazed crowds. Four daily newspapers are now published in "Change Square," as it is called, and about 20 weeklies.

The rebellions of the Arab Spring have been dealt devastating setbacks by coups, civil wars, and barbaric repression, but they showed that revolution and radical change are not just chapters in history books—if anything, the question of revolution is coming back to prominence in a world that is becoming increasingly economically and ecologically unstable. The lesson for us to draw is not that revolutions shouldn't happen—because they will—but that they have to go beyond replacing unjust regimes to replacing the undemocratic capitalist structures that put those regimes in power.

> I believe that the power of Corporate America, the power of Wall Street, the power of the drug companies, the power of the corporate media is so great that the only way we really transform America and do the things that the middle class and working class desperately need is through a political revolution, when millions of people begin to come together and stand up and say: our government is going to work for all of us, not just a handful of billionaires.

When Bernie Sanders made speeches like this during his campaign, he probably was using the R-word more as a rhetorical device than as a call to actually overthrow this system of government and replace it with something better. Let's take the suggestion seriously.

We really are up against an unelected and unenlightened oligarchy that can't even handle taxing itself to fix our collapsing bridges, much less rise to the historic challenge of preventing catastrophic climate change.

And now their hollowed-out democracy has made Donald Trump the most powerful person in the world. One of the biggest obstacles revolutionaries face is the fear of the unknown. Well, guess what? We're already there. So as we hurtle toward an uncertain future, we might as well fight like hell to make it ours.

Acknowledgments

Five years ago I wrote a draft for a strange little ebook called *America's Got Democracy! The Making of the World's Longest-Running Reality Show*. Knowing that it wouldn't be a big seller (and it wasn't), the people at Haymarket Books—and Dao X. Tran in particular—busted their butts to produce what became the starting point for the current book.

As for this book, dozens of people deserve a share of the blame, starting with the Haymarket crew led by Anthony Arnove and Julie Fain—and including Jim Plank, who didn't snap at me even after I changed the title for the seventh time, and the super-sharp copy editor Caroline Luft. Also thanks to Alan Maass and Ashley Dawson for giving valuable feedback on the draft, and Lee Wengraf and Llana Barber for being great writing buddies—as was Eric Ruder, who also designed the great cover that I strongly encourage people to judge the book by.

On a more general note, I'm grateful to many comrades in the International Socialist Organization who have taught me ideas to make sense of the world and the humility to adjust when the world doesn't cooperate with our theories. And I'm beyond grateful to have an incredible family: my delightful sister Jess and soon-to-be brother-in-law Chris (no backing out now), who also gave feedback on the draft; my relative-with-no-official-title Jeff, who I've been learning from since I was eight (but with the mind of a nine-year-old); and my incredible parents Stephanie, Fred, and Michael, who have been irresponsibly supportive of me even when I'm clearly clueless. It was Michael's illness in 2012 that indirectly led me to become a writer, and his recovery has been one of the miracles of my life.

Finally, finally, finally, there are the brilliant, beautiful, and hilarious women who have to live with me: Lila, who keeps me humble, Nadine, who keeps me on my toes, and Lucy, who has had such a profound impact on my life and personality that I sometimes don't know where I end and she begins—until she tells me to back off.

Index